THE HAMPTON READER

Published by *Iskra Books* © 2024

10 9 8 7 6 5 4 3 2 1

All rights reserved.
The moral rights of the author have been asserted.

ISKRA BOOKS
WWW.ISKRABOOKS.ORG
US | ENGLAND | IRELAND

Iskra Books is an independent scholarly publisher—publishing original works of revolutionary theory, history, education, and art, as well as edited collections, new translations, and critical republications of older works.

ISBN-13: 979-8-3302-7035-4 (*Softcover*)

British Library Cataloguing in Publication Data
A catalogue record for this book is available from the British Library.

Library of Congress Cataloguing-in-Publication Data
A catalog record for this book is available from the Library of Congress

Cover Art, Typesetting, and Design by BEN STAHNKE
Editing and Proofing by SRIHARI NAGESWARAN
Interior Cover Photography by DANIELA ORTIZ

THE HAMPTON READER

FROM THE ACADEMY TO THE STREETS

Notes from a
Working Class
Think Tank

Edited by
Colin Jenkins

iskra books

Contents

EDITORIAL PREFACE IX
Colin Jenkins

SECTION 1: POLITICS AND LIBERATORY STRUGGLE

1. WALTER RODNEY'S REVOLUTIONARY PRAXIS 1
D. Musa Springer

2. THE CASE FOR PROLETARIAN MULTINATIONAL UNITY 13
Nino Brown

SECTION 2: ARTS AND CULTURE

3. *SIN FRONTERAS*: DISPATCHES FROM MEXICO CITY 25
David A. Romero

4. ANTI-ABLEIST TEACHING STRATEGIES AND DISABILITY LIFE PHOTOGRAPHY 34
Sarah Pfohl

5. ARCHITECTURAL UTOPIAS: THE PEDAGOGY OF STILL-EXISTING SOCIALIST INFRASTRUCTURE 55
Derek R. Ford

SECTION 3: THEORIES, STRATEGIES, TACTICS

6. HISTORICAL MATERIALISM: A POSTDIGITAL PHILOSOPHICAL METHOD 73
Summer Pappachen

7. UNITING THE DIVIDED CONCEPT OF THE UNITED FRONT: A BRIEF HISTORY 88
Nicholas Stender

8. THEORETICAL AND PRACTICAL SELF-DETERMINATION OF INDIGENOUS NATIONS IN THE SOVIET UNION 102
Nolan Long

9. CORNEL WEST, THE PITFALLS OF BOURGEOIS POLITICS, AND FORGING A NEW FUTURE AMONG THE RUBBLE 113
Colin Jenkins

SECTION 4: THE STRUGGLE OVER SUBJECTIVITY

10. PRIDE MEANS FIGHT BACK: NOTES ON THE PERSISTENCE OF LGBTQ OPPRESSION 135
Alla Ivanchikova

11. SPEAKING LIKE CHILDREN: LINGUISTIC EXODUS FROM CAPITALIST SUBJECT-FORMATION 151
Richard M. Allen

12. DEMANDING TO BE: TRANS YOUTH AND CLASS STRUGGLE 166
Eli J. Pine

12. PARTING THOUGHTS—ATTACKING DIFFERENCE, PURSUING UNITY: BUILDING A SOCIALIST MOVEMENT AMIDST A DYNAMIC WORKING CLASS 179
Sudip Bhattacharya

EDITORIAL PREFACE

Colin Jenkins

COLIN JENKINS is founding editor of the *Hampton Institute*. His work has been featured in *Black Agenda Report, Truthout, Truthdig, Monthly Review, Counterpunch, Transnational Institute, Z Magazine, Dissident Voice, Popular Resistance*, and other people's media outlets. They've also published in *Social Justice: A Journal of Crime, Conflict, and World Order*, among other places.

WHEN THE HAMPTON INSTITUTE officially launched in May of 2013, the US was in the beginning stages of what seemed to be a socialist resurgence. We identified the need for a working-class think tank composed of and organized by organic intellectuals and organizers from a variety of struggles and backgrounds. Occupy Wall Street had spent a few years recalibrating the national political narrative toward class analysis. Bernie Sanders ramped up working-class causes against "big business" and "corporate greed" in Congress and, for the first time in decades, a major socialist publication (*Jacobin* Magazine) began to penetrate the mainstream. And finally, from 2015 to 2021, the Democratic Socialists of America (DSA) experienced a membership increase from 6,200 to 95,000, leading to several political candidates running under the DSA banner in local elections.

However, as exciting and necessary as this rebirth of class-conscious politics has been, it has also been a mixed bag full of mirages, setbacks, contradictions, confusion, and in-fighting. Ultimately, what appeared to be a socialist resurgence at first started to move into something resembling a social-democratic resurgence; or, in other words, a slight shift back toward the traditional liberalism of FDR, the Kennedys, LBJ, and New Deal/Great Society rhetoric. Occupy Wall Street eventually died due to an inability to channel its energy into a disciplined organizing force, which made it an easy target for the police raids ordered by then-president Obama to destroy encampments across the country. There are socialist groupings still tethered to the capitalist/imperialist Democrat Party under the assumption they and their publications can influence one of the two parties in this one-party imperialist state. Some publications often thus slip into anti-communist territory and generally lack a coherent anti-imperialist orientation. And, despite building a formidable organization through his electoral run for president, Bernie Sanders ultimately sold out, endorsed corporate candidates like Hillary Clinton and Joe Biden, and instructed his mass of supporters to do the same (although not everyone followed his instructions).

So, while the term "socialism" has become more acceptable in its usage, it has often been used in a manner that is completely detached from the crucial scientific orientation of Marxism. This misuse and/or confusion can be narrowed down to three main causes: (1) residual fears that remain from the Cold War era and the US's history of brutality against communists, (2) ruling-class propaganda that has conditioned so many people to falsely believe the United States is a country that operates on an honest foundation of democracy, individual rights, and freedoms, and (3) a severe lack of education, especially regarding history, historical processes, and even the most basic understandings of systems like capitalism and socialism. In other words: fear, propaganda, and miseducation.

Instead of understanding capitalism as the latest epoch of human exploitation, too many view it as the "end of history." Instead of understanding the struggle between the capitalist class and working class as the primary force on society, many believe in class collaboration. Instead of understanding that we must force capitalism to give way to socialism, just as feudalism gave way to capitalism, too many yearn for ways to tame the system and make its oppressive structure more palatable. Instead of realizing the pitfalls inherent in electoral politics, especially in this corporate-fascistic stage of monopoly capitalism, many continue to throw vast amounts of attention, energy, and resources into "progressive" campaigns.

The *Hampton Institute* itself has experienced its own contradictions and inconsistencies over the years, at times regretfully publishing analyses that could, at best, potentially be construed as counter-revolutionary and/or anti-communist. We did so alongside polemics taking an opposing stance, however, although this was at first a matter of spontaneity rather than intentionality. And while such intent has surely never existed, we would be foolish to pretend it was the result of anything other than the horizontalist and more anarchist form of our publication. Such is the nature of revolutionary politics. From individuals to organizations, we all experience our own processes of political education and ideological development. We attempt to apply theory to real-world situations, only to find unexpected barriers. We attempt to discard theory in certain real-world scenarios only to find we inevitably lose our focus in doing so. This truly is a layered process rife with lessons, regrets, indecisions, and uncertainties.

While there is little doubt that most have good intentions, good intentions are simply not enough in 2024. The sober reality is we are knee-deep in a very rapid descent from covert fascism to overt fascism as the capitalist system is a rotting corpse on life support, like something of a Frankenstein. Capitalists and their ruling-classes worldwide seem content to let the world burn, quite literally. So, the working-class masses are the only hope for humanity. And the key to becoming a formidable power to challenge this descent is not only found in our processes of political education and ideological development, but also in collective action, in discipline, in militancy, in formulating a plan and purpose within an organization, alongside other socialists and communists.

The *Hampton Institute* exists to serve a role in the ideological war, which is a necessary precursor to collective action. As we have all been systematically attacked with miseducation and propaganda from ruling-class curriculum and mass media—sources that have interests that are not only diametrically opposed to ours but feed off our oppression—a counterattack is needed. Therefore, we must create and maintain our own avenues of working-class education and ideological development to counter this. As Paulo Freire brilliantly noted: "No pedagogy which is truly liberating can remain distant from the oppressed by treating them as unfortunates and by presenting for their emulation models from among the oppressors. The oppressed must be their own example in the struggle for their redemption."[1] In other words, proletarian edu-

---

1   Paulo Freire, *Pedagogy of the Oppressed*, trans. M.B. Ramos (New York: Con-

cation is inherently liberatory, whereas bourgeois education is, by design, oppressive.

Understanding that our lowly, *structural* position in the capitalist system is necessary for the system and its owning class to thrive allows us to recapture reality from the haze of capitalist conditioning. Understanding this position which has been sold to us is not *natural* allows us the fortitude to embrace the class struggle that we were born into, that our parents were born into, that our children were born into. And, most importantly, understanding this class struggle as the foundation that binds the working class together allows us to recognize forms of compounded oppression that exist for hyper-targeted members of the working class—black, brown, women, disabled, LGBTQ, those in the global south, indigenous, etc.—without giving in to the divisiveness created by liberal/capitalist forms of identity politics and culture wars.

The following text, *From the Academy to the Streets: Notes from a Working-Class Think Tank*, is a wonderful collection of essays, most of which are original or heavily modified, that get to the heart of our class struggle. The team of contributors who have poured their hearts and souls into this body of work are, quite simply, a powerhouse of proletarian educators, activists, and thinkers. No text or book is the product of an individual or even a single organization, and the *Institute* and the texts that comprise this new volume owe much to our collaborations with similar groupings, from the *Critical Theory Workshop* and *Monthly Review* to *Liberation School* and *Black Agenda Report*. More directly, the determined, committed, and brilliant comrades at *Iskra Books* have been a godsend for those of us at the *Hampton Institute*. The quality and integrity of their work is unmatched, and we are honored to release this text under their label.

Enjoy. Prepare. Embrace revolutionary optimism in the face of despair. All power to the people.

COLIN JENKINS, *Hampton Institute*
February 29, 2024

---

tinuum, 1970/2000), 54.

SECTION 1
Politics & Liberatory Struggle

CHAPTER 1
WALTER RODNEY'S REVOLUTIONARY PRAXIS

D. Musa Springer

D. MUSA SPRINGER is a cultural worker, community organizer, and independent researcher. They are a member of the Walter Rodney Foundation, host of the Groundings podcast, an editor at Hood Communist. Springer's most recent publication is *Alive and Paranoid* (Iskra, 2024).

DEREK R. FORD: Thanks so much for agreeing to this interview, Musa. I always look forward to working and learning with you and I appreciate your work on revolutionary movements and education. I know you're involved with the Walter Rodney Foundation, which is not just about preserving his legacy but promoting the revolutionary theories, practices, and models he developed. Can you tell me a bit about the Foundation, your role, and why it's important for the movement broadly in the U.S.?

D. MUSA SPRINGER: The Walter Rodney Foundation was formed by the Rodney family in 2006, with the goal of sharing Walter Rodney's life and works with students, scholars, activists, and communities around the world. Because of the example Walter Rodney left in his own personal life and the principles he established in his work, we see supporting grassroots movements, offering public education, and the praxis of advancing social justice in a number of ways as what it really means to share his life with the world; Walter Rodney was as much a fan of *doing* as he was speaking, after all. We have a number of annual programs, including many political education classes oriented around themes related to Rodney's body of work—colonialism, underdevelopment, Pan-African struggle, scholar-activism, assassination, Black history, the Caribbean, etc. We also run ongoing projects like the Legacies Project, which is actively seeking and collecting stories and oral histories around the world about Walter Rodney.

I've volunteered with the WRF since around 2013. I currently help coordinate the Foundation's social media, and offer other types of support as needed.

I feel the Foundation is crucial for the movement broadly for a number of reasons. First, the critical analysis of slavery, colonialism, imperialism, and underdevelopment Rodney gave in works like *How Europe Underdeveloped Africa* remains relevant, and we need organizations dedicated to distilling this knowledge. Second, because our movement must reckon with the lives, works, histories, struggles, and relevance of the elders past and present who we owe so much to, whether it's the Claudia Jones School For Political Education, the Paul Robeson House & Museum, Habana's *Centro Martin Luther King Jr.*, or the Walter Rodney Foundation, there needs to be organizations and groups dedicated to maintaining these legacies and continuing their work.

More than just maintaining legacies, in other words, the WRF also makes sure that Walter Rodney's critical analyses remain critical and do not get co-opted. Finally, the foundation is important because it is run by the Rodney family, who themselves have extensive decades of organizing, advocacy, and knowledge which is always beneficial. (And I must clarify, whenever I speak of a "movement" broadly as above, I am speaking about the global Black Liberation Movement foremost, in a Revolutionary Pan-Africanist sense).

FORD: Those are precisely the reasons we wanted to do this interview, particularly to expose readers (and ourselves) to the broader range and context of his work and to learn more about the depth of his praxis and why it's needed today. To start then, can you give our readers a bit of historical and biographical context for Walter Rodney's life and work? What was happening at the time, who was he working with, agitating against, etc.?

SPRINGER: I will try to be brief here and give some basic biographical information, because there's so much one could say. Walter Rodney was an activist, intellectual, husband, and father, who lived and visited everywhere from Guyana, Jamaica, the USSR, Cuba, Tanzania, Kenya, Uganda, Ghana, Britain, Spain, Portugal, Italy, the U.S., and Canada. He was born in Georgetown, Guyana in March 1942, where he was raised and resided for much of his life. He graduated from the University of the West Indies (UWI) in Jamaica in 1963, then received his PhD with honors in African History from the School of Oriental and African Studies in London at the age of 24. His thesis, *A History of the Upper Guinea Coast, 1545-1800*, was completed in 1966 and then published in 1970, and I highly recommend it to readers.[1]

Rodney was deeply influenced by a number of revolutionary movements and ideologies which had flourished during his lifetime: the multitude of armed African decolonial struggles across the continent, the Black Power Movement in the U.S., Third World revolutionaries like Che, Mao, and Cabral, and Pan-African/Marxist praxis generally. Walter Rodney taught in Jamaica, working to break the bourgeois academy from its ivory tower, where he delivered a number of *groundings* across the island to the working class, including the Rastafari and other marginalized communities at the time. While at the 1968 Black Writers' Conference in Montreal, Canada, the Jamaican government banned him from re-entering on the grounds that his 'associations' with Cuban, Soviet, and other communist governments posed a threat to Jamaica's national security. Massive outbursts now known as the "Rodney Riots" subsequently broke out across Kingston. Rodney spent many months writing in Cuba prior to traveling to the University of Dar es Salaam in revolutionary Tanzania in 1969.

In 1974, Walter returned to Guyana to take up an appointment as Professor of History at the University of Guyana, but the government (under the dictates of President Forbes Burnham) rescinded the appointment. Rodney remained in Guyana and helped form the socialist political party, the Working People's Alliance, alongside activist-intellectuals like Eusi Kwayana and Andaiye. Between 1974 and 1979 he emerged as the leading figure in the resistance movement against the increasingly repressive government led by the People's National Congress, which can be summarized as publicly espousing Pan-African, anti-apartheid, and socialist talking points while running a despotic, cor-

---

1   Rodney A. Walter, *A History of the Upper Guinea Coast, 1545-1800*, PhD dissertation (University of London, 1966). Available at: https://eprints.soas.ac.uk/31255/1/Rodney_History_Upper_Guinea_Coast.pdf.

rupt Western-backed state operation.

He gave public and private talks all over the country that served to engender a new political consciousness in the country, and he stated in his speeches and writing that he believed a people's revolution was the only way towards true liberation for the Guyanese people. During this period he developed and advocated the WPA's politics of "People's Power" that called on the broad masses of people to take political control instead of a tiny clique, and "multiracial democracy" to address the steep obstacles presented by the racial disunity between Afro-Guyanese and Indo-Guyanese peoples (which is still present today).

On June 13, 1980, shortly after returning from independence celebrations in Zimbabwe, Rodney was assassinated in Georgetown, Guyana by an explosive device hidden in a walkie-talkie, given to him by Gregory Smith, former sergeant in the Guyana Defense Force. Smith was subsequently given new passports and secretly flown out of the country. Donald Rodney, Walter's younger brother who was in the car with him when the bomb went off, was falsely accused and convicted of being in possession of explosives; he fought to clear his own name for decades until April of this year, when Guyana's appellate court exonerated him. A few weeks later the Government of Guyana officially recognized Walter's death as an assassination. This comes after years of struggle on behalf of the Rodney family, particularly Dr. Patricia Rodney and the WRF. Walter was just 38 years old at the time of his assassination, but his legacy is continued by his wife, three children, and the dozens of incredible speeches, essays, interviews, and books he gave and wrote.

FORD: Rodney's best-known work is *How Europe Underdeveloped Africa*. Why do you think that is? What are his main arguments there and are they still relevant to understanding Western imperialism and African resistance?

SPRINGER: That's a special type of book that, like few others, can completely change or deeply influence one's politics. Rodney essentially put forth a historical materialist argument showing that economically, politically, and socially, Europe was in a dialectical relationship with Africa, wherein the wealth of Europe was *dependent upon* the underdevelopment of Africa. In other words, Rodney shows with painstaking detail how European capitalism (and eventually the global capitalist system) could not have existed without the systematic pre-colonial exploitation of Africa, the massive amounts of capital generated through the Maafa, later the expansive economic, political, financial, and social domination under direct colonial rule, and the continuing—or perfecting—of these exploitative processes under the current neo-colonial world order. As Rodney puts it:

Colonialism was not merely a system of exploitation, but one whose essential purpose was to repatriate the profits to the so-called mother country. From an African viewpoint, that amounted to consistent expatriation of surplus produced by African labor out of African resources. *It meant the development of Europe as part of the same dialectical process in which Africa was underdeveloped.*[2]

It remains his most recognized work because it remains incredibly relevant, both in the sense that the current world capitalist structure is built on this historical underdevelopment of the South, and because, under imperialism, the North must still exploit and perpetually underdevelop the South. Its publication marked a significant contribution to theories of underdevelopment and dependency. Alongside revolutionary intellectuals like Samir Amin and Osagyefo Kwame Nkrumah, it was groundbreaking in that it applied Marxism to the Third World with great precision and depth. Further, Rodney goes into detail about not just underdevelopment but the history of class society and feudalism in Africa, social violence, fascism, agrarian struggles, racism, enslavement, gender, economics, misleadership and African sellouts, and so much more. In some ways, I like to think of it as a foundational text for revolutionaries in the same way that many consider Marx's *Capital* or Marx and Engels' *The Communist Manifesto* to be.

One example of its relevance is in thinking about labor and the workforce as it relates to slavery. Rodney uses data to explain that the social violence of the Maafa had a deep impact on African development because it removed millions of young Africans from the labor force, created technological regression, and directed whatever mass energy aimed at productive or technological innovation towards the trade in human captives.

---

2   Walter Rodney, *How Europe Underdeveloped Africa* (Cambridge: Harvard University Press, 1972/1982), 149.

He says, "The European slave trade was a direct block, in removing millions of youth and young adults who are the human agents from whom inventiveness springs. Those who remained in areas badly hit by slave capturing were preoccupied about their freedom rather than with improvements in production."[3] I relate this to the crisis of incarceration in the U.S., wherein millions of Africans are removed from the labor force, removed from their families and communities, and in the same way, are removed even from the very opportunity of innovation and production to instead perform hyper-exploited, forced labor at the hands of the settler-capitalist state. Ruth Wilson Gilmore's work has, to an extent, explained how the capitalist state necessitates this incarceration, and in the same way I'd suggest that European capitalism's violently expansive nature necessitated the multitude of exploitative interactions with Africa, from slavery to neo-colonialism.

FORD: That kind of theoretical engagement and empirical investigation is always crucial and, for me, a fundamental aspect of Marxism or Leninism, as both are historical through and through and, thus, dynamic and contingent on place, space, and social formation. I am wondering what influence it had, not just academically, but in terms of revolutionary struggles?

SPRINGER: I get letters, emails, and calls almost on a monthly basis from incarcerated people who are reading not only that book but also *The Groundings With My Brothers*, an underrated gem of Rodney's. They've formed reading groups and created zines around his work; asked me to further explain concepts he mentions; and even drawn incredible illustrations of Rodney. I find this engagement with Rodney equally valuable (and often more rewarding) as that of academics. Patricia Rodney has told me that over the decades incarcerated people have consistently gravitated towards Rodney's work and written to her, likely because of the accessible way he's able to break down complex concepts. I'm actually currently working with the WRF on a project to donate many copies of Walter Rodney's books to incarcerated people, and hopefully, in the coming months we'll have more info to share on this.

Beyond that, Rodney's work has globally influenced the left in more ways than I could explain or speculate in this interview. His revolution-

---

3   Ibid., 105.

ary African analysis has corrected Eurocentric views of history and allowed us to better understand the important role decolonization plays in our fight against imperialism. He also offers a great example for young writers, researchers, and organizers on how to write materialist history and analyses. For example, as one reads his work it's impossible not to note the multitude of ways Rodney directly eviscerates bourgeois historians and apologists.

FORD: Please keep us updated on the WRF project, because we'll definitely want to support it. It seems that Rodney was exemplary at achieving true "praxis," the merging of theory and practice. One of the ways this shows up most is in his pedagogical work—his theories and practices—which he called "groundings." It's not just a pedagogy, but a practice of decolonizing knowledge and empowering oppressed people to organize, at least as I understand it. I know it's influenced your own work and you've written about it, so how would you describe it to someone just joining the struggle, or just learning about imperialism, colonialism, and racism?

SPRINGER: Yes, I co-wrote a piece titled "Groundings: A Revolutionary Pan-African Pedagogy for Guerilla Intellectuals" that's available for free online, and which I plan to re-write/expand soon, and my podcast is named after this pedagogical model as well. Usually, when people refer to Rodney's "groundings" they are referring to his period as a professor in Jamaica, where he quite literally broke away from the elitist academy and brought his lectures to the people: in the streets, the yards, the slums, wherever workers and others gathered. He gave public lectures on African and Caribbean history, political movements, capitalism, colonialism, Black Power, etc. These groundings were often based on what people expressed interest in learning about, and Rodney found ways to make various topics relevant and important to the lives of those listening. In many regards, Rodney should be placed next to popular educators like Paulo Freire for his contributions and his example of merging theory with practice. The book *The Groundings With My Brothers* is a collection of speeches, many given at or about these groundings.[4]

More than just giving public lectures, groundings entailed democ-

---

4 Walter Rodney, *The Groundings with my Brothers*, ed. J.J. Benjamin and A.T. Rodney (New York: Verso, 1969/2019).

ratizing knowledge and the tools of knowledge production, which are traditionally tied up with the capitalist academy. He empowered communities to tap into their own histories, oral and written, to generate knowledge and research amongst themselves based on their interests and needs, to place European history and Eurocentric frameworks as non-normative, and to hold African history as crucially important to the process of African revolution. He brilliantly lays out the importance of African history in Black liberation in "African History in the Service of Black Liberation," a speech he gave in Montreal, ironically at the conference from which he would not be allowed to return to Jamaica.[5]

In the most basic terms, I would explain groundings as the act of coming together in a group, explaining, discussing, and exploring topics relevant to the group's lives; everyone in the group listens, engages, contributes, reasons, and *grounds* with one another, and all voices are valued. Groundings can take place inside of jail cells, within classrooms, in parks and workplaces, or anywhere the intentions of Afrocentric group dialogue and learning are maintained.

FORD: One of the interesting things about *The Groundings With My Brothers* is the way it moves from Black Power in the U.S. to Jamaica, to the West Indies, to Africa, and then to groundings. As a final set of questions, can you explain what he meant by Black Power and Blackness, and what they had to do with education?

SPRINGER: Well, to understand that book you have to understand a bit about the context in which the book arose. In *Groundings* we see Rodney's ability to take seemingly large concepts like neo-colonialism, Black Power, Blackness, etc., and break them down to a level that could engage people. It taught them how to make sense of the fact that the people oppressing them were the same color and nationality as them. In the midst of decolonization and independence movements sweeping the world, there was a crucial Cold War and neo-colonization taking place simultaneously. Facilitating this counter-revolution were several African leaders and activists employed to do the bidding of imperialist powers seeking

---

5   Walter Rodney, (1968). "African History in the Service of Black Liberation," Congress of Black Writers, Montreal, Canada, 12 October 1968. Available here: referenced from *History is a Weapon*, undated, available here: https://www.historyisaweapon.com/defcon1/rodneylib.html.

to regain or retain their power. In Jamaica, this was no different: the Jamaican government in 1968 went so far as to ban any literature printed in the USSR and Cuba, as well as an extensive list of works about Black Power and Black revolution, including those of Black Power activists such as Trinidadian-born Kwame Ture (Stokley Carmichael), Malcolm X, and Elijah Muhammad.

Placed in this context, we see that Rodney's work explaining the U.S. Black Power movement's importance and relevance for the Caribbean and Africans everywhere was quite important in raising the political consciousness of working-class Africans. A key part of this was educating on the role of "indigenous lackeys" or "local lackeys of imperialism" in maintaining the (neo)colonial status quo. In a speech initially published as a pamphlet titled, *Yes to Marxism!*, he says:

When I was in Jamaica in 1960, I would say that already my consciousness of West Indian society was not that we needed to fight the British but that we needed to fight the British, the Americans, and their indigenous lackeys. That I see as an anti-neo-colonial consciousness as distinct from a purely anti-colonial consciousness.[6]

His distinct analysis of misleadership and its colonial implications was a searing threat, as Dr. Charisse Burden-Stelly wonderfully explains.[7]

Rodney defines power as being kept "milky white" through imperialist forces of violence, exploitation, and discrimination, and that Black Power, in contrast, may be seen as the antithesis to this imperialist, colonial, racial demarcation that structures capitalist society. The following quote is long, but I want to quote it in full because I find it useful. He says:

The present Black Power movement in the United States is a rejection of hopelessness and the policy of doing nothing to halt the oppression of blacks by whites. It recognises the absence of Black Power, but is confident of the potential of Black Power on this globe. Marcus

---

6   Cited in Charisse Burden-Stelly, "Between Radicalism and Repression: Walter Rodney's Revolutionary Praxis," *Black Perspectives*, 06 May 2019. Available here: https://www.aaihs.org/between-radicalism-and-repression-walter-rodneys-revolutionary-praxis/.

7   Ibid.

Garvey was one of the first advocates of Black Power and is still today the greatest spokesman ever to have been produced by the movement of black consciousness. 'A race without power and authority is a race without respect,' wrote Garvey. He spoke to all Africans on the earth, whether they lived in Africa, South America, the West Indies or North America, and he made blacks aware of their strength when united. The USA was his main field of operation, after he had been chased out of Jamaica by the sort of people who today pretend to have made him a hero. All of the black leaders who have advanced the cause in the USA since Garvey's time have recognised the international nature of the struggle against white power. Malcolm X, our martyred brother, became the greatest threat to white power in the USA because he began to seek a broader basis for his efforts in Africa and Asia, and he was probably the first individual who was prepared to bring the race question in the US up before the UN as an issue of international importance. The Students Nonviolent Coordinating Committee (SNCC), the important Black Power organisation, developed along the same lines; and at about the same time that the slogan Black Power came into existence a few years ago, SNCC was setting up a foreign affairs department, headed by James Foreman, who afterwards travelled widely in Africa. [Kwame Ture] has held serious discussions in Vietnam, Cuba and the progressive African countries, such as Tanzania and Guinea. These are all steps to tap the vast potential of power among the hundreds of millions of oppressed black peoples.[8]

He defined Black Power in the U.S. context as "when decisions are taken in the normal day-to-day life of the USA, the interests of the blacks must be taken into account *out of respect for their power*—power that can be used destructively if it is not allowed to express itself constructively. This is what Black Power means in the particular conditions of the USA."[9]

Rodney finds there are three ways in which Black Power applies to the West Indies: "(1) the break with imperialism which is historically white racist; (2) the assumption of power by the black masses in the islands; (3) the cultural reconstruction of the society in the image of the

---

8   Rodney, *The Groundings with my Brothers*, 14-15.

9   Ibid., 18.

blacks."[10]

I'm sure this was a much longer answer than anticipated, but I find it incredibly important to understand that Walter Rodney's conception of Black Power was revolutionary, and was also fundamentally inspired by his Marxist approach which sought to apply these revolutionary ideals to the specific context of the Caribbean and Africans globally.

He also explains, in detail, his notion of "Blackness" as being stretched differently to how we conceive of "Blackness" today so as to include the entirety of the colonized world. He states, "The black people of whom I speak, therefore, are non-whites—the hundreds of millions of people whose homelands are in Asia and Africa, with another few millions in the Americas;" however he clarifies that "further subdivision can be made with reference to all people of African descent, whose position is clearly more acute than that of most nonwhite groups."[11]

He places Blackness as the most crucial element, stating "Black Power is a doctrine about black people, for black people, preached by black people," and later adds that "once a person is said to be black by the white world, then that is usually the most important thing about him; fat or thin, intelligent or stupid, criminal or sportsman – these things pale into insignificance."[12]

Frantz Fanon makes a similar move when he states: "In the colonies, the economic infrastructure is also a superstructure. The cause is the effect: You are rich because you are white, you are white because you are rich. This is why a Marxist analysis should always be slightly stretched when it comes to addressing the colonial issue."[13]

FORD: It wasn't longer than it needed to be, and it was incredibly informative. The context you've given has helped me grasp his moves throughout that book and his project and vision in general. It's important that while stretching "Blackness" he didn't muddy it but rather sharpened it, which helps me understand his insistence that the Cuban

---

10   Ibid., 24.

11   Ibid., 10.

12   Ibid., 9, 10.

13   Fanon, Frantz. (1961/2005). *The Wretched of the Earth*, trans. R. Philcox (New York: Grove Press), 5.

Revolution was a Black Power revolt against white power even as "Black Cubans fought alongside white Cuban workers and peasants."[14] I've really appreciated your time and energy, and definitely recommend that our readers check out your podcast and other work. I'm looking forward to our next collaboration!

---

14   Rodney, *The Groundings with My Brothers*, 27.

CHAPTER 2
THE CASE FOR PROLETARIAN MULTINATIONAL UNITY
Nino Brown

NINO BROWN is an educator, anti-war activist, and organizer. In addition to publishing in both academic and popular outlets such as *Black Agenda Report*, *Monthly Review*, and *Philosophy of Education*, Brown edited the book *Revolutionary Education: Theory and Practice for Socialist Organizers* (Liberation Media, 2022). He is a former public school teacher and rank and file labor organizer with the Boston Teachers Union. Additionally, he is a member of the Jericho Movement, a movement formed by political prisoners to free all political prisoners and prisoners of war.

Introduction

DESPITE WHAT RULING CLASS U.S. politicians say, the U.S. has never been "one nation," nor does it provide "liberty and justice for all."[1] It is an empire. In order to maintain itself as an empire, the ruling class divides the working class by 'race' and other social constructs. Black Americans exist neither as a "race" nor "workers who just so happened to be Black"; rather, to borrow W.E.B. DuBois' phrase, Black Americans constitute a "nation within a nation." We are a captive nation, and a distinct group of people oppressed by the U.S. empire. As Malcolm X so cogently put it:

> I don't even consider myself an American. If you and I were Americans, there'd be no problem [...] I'm not going to sit at your table and watch you eat, with nothing on my plate, and call myself a diner. Sitting at the table doesn't make you a diner, unless you eat some of what's on that plate [...] I'm speaking as a victim of this American system. And I see America through the eyes of the victim. I don't see any

---

1   Lindsay, Peta. (2014). "Is the United States One Nation?," *Liberation School*, June 30. Available online at: https://www.liberationschool.org/is-the-united-states-one-nation/.

American dream; I see an American nightmare.[2]

Contrary to the liberal notion that Black people suffer because of outdated attitudes, beliefs, and practices, Marxists understand that the oppression of the Black nation in the US has a material basis. More importantly, we understand the historical role of the Black nation in the revolutionary traditions of this land, as Black people have consistently led the class struggle for democracy and for socialism. What distinguishes Black people as a nation is that they are bound by a common culture, history, shared traditions and customs, occupy a contiguous territory, and most importantly, share a culture rooted in political economy.

There is a material basis for proletarian multinational unity—internationally and within the U.S.—which cannot be meaningfully understood or acted upon without analyzing the specific and necessary role of Black liberation struggles. This view is in contradistinction to the notion that the white working class has a "material interest" in the maintenance of capitalism and imperialism or that white people are hopelessly "bought off." The article posits that the struggle for Black liberation is among the sharpest class struggles under capitalism, is a harbinger of unity, and examines historical justifications for these claims by offering an account of class struggle and focusing on Reconstruction.

Formation of the Black Nation

The formation of African Americans in this country must be properly understood if we are to truly strike at the roots of racism: Black people are an oppressed nation, and an exploited class, and thus our fight is largely shaped by the logics of white supremacy and capitalist exploitation of our labor.

Black people were forged into a separate nation by our particular history, our shared experience in the United States, tracing back to the earliest forms of capitalism in the U.S., which grew rapidly through the plantation system in the pre-Civil War South. The plantation system relied upon chattel slave labor to produce agricultural profits from the land ruthlessly stolen by the early colonists through the genocide

---

2   X, Malcolm. (1965). "The Ballot or the Bullet," in *Malcolm X Speaks*, George Breitman, ed. (Grove Press).

of many Native Americans and the forced displacement and dispossession from their ancestral homelands. Millions of Africans from different regions of the continent were brutally kidnapped and brought to the U.S to work on the lands, till the soil, build capital, and bear the lash of colonial oppression.

Our kidnapped ancestors spoke different languages, practiced different religions, had different cultures, engaged in separate economic activities and came from distinct tribes and nations before European colonization and enslavement. White slave traders abruptly stole them from their rich social and economic lives and sold them into slavery. In the U.S., enslaved Africans were thus forged into a new nation, a subjugated Black nation, like our Chicano, Native American, and Puerto Rican family.

The question of racism, white supremacy, and ultimately national oppression stem from historical and social marcations and not biological ones. The solution to Black oppression cannot be found nor achieved without an understanding of the historical formation of the Black nation as a nation without a state, composed of primarily proletarians disenfranchised and dehumanized as a foundational platform for the development of U.S. capitalism. The displacement and genocide of Native Americans spurred the spread of the chattel slavery system and provided much of the initial material wealth for the U.S. ruling class. The creation of a distinct Black nation was thus fundamental to the development of capitalism in the United States, and it is also the ruling class' Achilles heel, the contradiction that is the "weakest link" in imperialism's chain of oppression. Slavery was the earliest form of institutionalized oppression of Black people in the U.S. Although plantation slavery no longer exists, the institutionalized oppression of Black people continues today. It is the struggle against the institutionalized oppression of the Black nation that has catalyzed larger class and democratic struggle in all periods of social upheaval and antagonism in the U.S.

The American capitalist system promotes the idea that racism is a "stain" on "American democracy" and that formal legal rights for Blacks should suffice in solving their problems. The U.S. ruling class knows that Black people are a "nation within a nation" and the struggle of Black people has historically united the multinational working class and directed its ire towards the ruling elite.

Black Liberation: A Materialist History

There is nothing magical about Black people or Black struggle that makes it a primary contradiction for the class struggle of the U.S. multinational working class. The answers as to why this struggle has historically played a vanguard role are to be found nowhere other than the history of the development of capitalism in this country and the particular role that Black labor played in shaping it.

The historical example of Radical Reconstruction illustrates both the potential of the Black struggle for liberation to unite the working class, and the lengths the ruling class will go to divide the working class against itself. In "Black Reconstruction," W.E.B. DuBois argues the period from 1865-1877 set a powerful example of "democratic government and the labor movement today," and that "the destruction of the slave power was the basis for real national unity and the further development of capitalism, which would produce conditions most favorable for the growth of the labor movement."[3] At no other time had members of the Black oppressed nation made such strident moves toward democracy and social justice. Although it was not a movement explicitly for socialism, it was a movement that swiftly abolished old colonial laws and empowered the Black community over the rights of the defeated class of slave-owners. Despite the fact that the proletarian movement would give rise to the industrialization of modern bourgeois society, Reconstruction was nonetheless an attack on landed property in general.

Ultimately, Radical Reconstruction was a period of extended Black political power over former masters, and what ensued was not "chaos," as bourgeois history has characterized the period, but actual progress. It was during these 12 years that Black people held some semblance of state power, and wielded it with a political line directly antagonistic to capital. Gains were made not only for freed slaves, but for working class white people as well, demonstrating that the relationship between national liberation, socialism, and the struggle for democracy are inseparable.

---

3   Allen, James. (1937). *Reconstruction: The Battle for Democracy 1865-1876*. (New York, International Publishers).

Like in every revolution, the military conflict of the Civil War was followed by a period in which remnants of the previous social order were suppressed, both by political means and by force. This is a necessary tactic in order to fight off the former ruling class's attempts to regain political power. How to suppress the enraged Confederate forces had been the subject of debate within Northern political circles throughout the war. On the one hand, moderates like Abraham Lincoln wanted to incorporate as many elements of the old slave-owning class into a new pro-Union government as possible. (Recall that Lincoln promised slave owners who cooperated with the federal government that they would be able to maintain "their property.") On the other hand, Radical Republicans favored harsh repression and exclusion of Confederate society from political power.

Ultimately, the Radical Republicans were the driving political force of the Reconstruction Era. In an objective sense, they were the revolutionary, unwavering and determined wing of the divided capitalist class. It is important to remember that though they were radical in their advocacy for the end of slavery, they were still part of the capitalist class. Their political base was in Congress, where they held a majority that grew in the years immediately following the Civil War. They understood that the freed slaves were the most solid base of support for the Union, considering Black people rejoiced at the military defeat of the Confederacy. Across the South, former slaves organized meetings and political organizations to take advantage of their new freedom.

In early 1865, just weeks before the Confederate surrender, the federal government created the Freedmen's Bureau. Under the military protection of Union troops, both Black and white, the Bureau organized a vast education project for former slaves—a project which laid the foundation for public education nationwide. And although it was impeded by inadequate funding, it nonetheless established medical aid, food rations, schools, colleges, industrial education and hospitals, ultimately aiding poverty-stricken whites in addition to former slaves. It was even authorized to carry out a land redistribution program, although such radical measures were never widely implemented.

The gains in the struggle for Black liberation would be rolled back almost as soon as they were instituted. President Andrew Johnson assumed the presidency following Lincoln's assassination, having posed during the war as a Radical. However, he quickly emerged as the leading force of political reaction within the national Republican Party and made his alliance with the white supremacist ideals of the Confederacy clear. After the defeat of the Confederacy, Johnson installed new governments in the Southern states made up wholly or primarily of pardoned ex-Confederates. And in late 1865, several of these legislatures, installed by Johnson himself, passed laws known as the "Black Codes."

The Black Codes varied from state to state, but had common features. Economically, the main thrust of the Black Codes was to re-institute the plantation system. They provided labor contracts for Black laborers, often with terms not much different than slavery, prohibiting Black people without proper papers from migrating from one state to another. The Black Codes also limited Black people's participation in politics with educational or property restrictions. In the eyes of many, the power of the former slavocracy was being restored, which was further empowered by Johnson's 1866 veto of an extension of the Freedmen's Bureau and a Civil Rights bill that would grant citizenship to Black people.

Black Reconstruction was a period of intense struggle among the people and within the ruling class. In 1866, new elections to the House of Representatives took place, and with the Southern states not yet readmitted to the Union, Radical Republicans made big gains, winning enough seats to override Johnson's vetoes. And as a result, the 10-year period beginning in 1867, known as "Radical Reconstruction," was a period of the most far-reaching social change ever to be seen in U.S. history.

In addition to the introduction of new social programs, the years following 1866 saw a rise in Black political power. In 1871, a Civil Rights Act, often called the Anti-Klan Act, was passed over Johnson's veto. The Act provided protection for the newly freed Black population by seeking to end the legalization of fascist terror directed at them. Under this law, which still stands today, equitable relief was made available to those whose constitutional rights had been violated by someone acting under state authority, by enabling the victim to sue. During Reconstruction, federal troops were used to enforce this law, and Klan members were prosecuted in Federal Court, in front of predominantly Black juries. As a result, hundreds of Klan members were fined and imprisoned, resulting in the destruction of the KKK in South Carolina, and a significant weakening of it in the rest of the region. This is an example of what can happen when the state itself is not upheld by racist violence—oppressed people see real justice. As Frederick Douglass said, speaking to the Anti-Klan Act of 1871, "The law on the side of freedom is of great advantage only when there is power to make that law respected."

The Reconstruction Act put the whole former Confederacy under military control and forced the creation of new state governments in accord with voting rights for Black people. Black people organized into Union Leagues in order to exert their political power, and over 1,500 were elected to office during Reconstruction, further catalyzing programs of expanded social, educational, economic, and political rights. It was to be expected that with each step forward for the newly emancipated Black people, racist violence would increase; and it did.

Met with extreme violence from the Ku Klux Klan, Black people defended themselves and the gains of emancipation through mass campaigns and with arms in hand. Regiments of Black soldiers patrolled the streets throughout the South, an image parallel to that of the Black Panther Party for Self Defense almost 100 years later. However, the weight of the racist whites' organizations proved to be too powerful for the Black community to overcome, especially as support for Reconstruction waned in the North.

Racists sought to disarm the Black masses. Throughout the Southern states and neighboring regions, gun control laws were introduced—but selectively only applied to the Black population, who relied on their guns to defend themselves.

And then, in 1877, Republican president-elect Rutherford B. Hayes agreed to what became known as the Compromise of 1876, or in the Black community as the "Great Betrayal of 1876." It was under this compromise that Hayes and the Republicans agreed to remove all remaining federal troops from the South, in exchange for the Republicans retaining the White House.

A reign of KKK terror and lynching enveloped the South as the

Northern troops were removed. The dictatorship of the Reconstruction period, with the old slave owners repressed and the former slaves living in a semi-democracy, was replaced by the reintroduction of the old dictatorship of the slavocracy.

So we find that in 1877, the Northern capitalist establishment decisively turned their backs on Reconstruction, striking a deal with the old slavocracy to return the South to white supremacist rule in exchange for the South's acceptance of Northern capitalist expansion. The industrial capitalists made peace with the defeated slavocracy at the cost of many concessions—the easiest for them being the aspirations of the Black working classes.

The first real experience of Black political power in the U.S.—coming after centuries of attempted slave insurrections and resistance—was ultimately defeated. But although subjected to renewed and constant terrorism from the forces of white supremacy, the Black freedom movement could not be extinguished. Generation after generation found new methods of struggle.

"America is a Powder Keg" and Black Liberation is the "Detonating Factor"

Under capitalism, all workers are exploited by capital, albeit at different rates and degrees of intensity. Most Black people in the U.S. are working class; like the vast majority of humanity, we have nothing but our labor power to sell. Throughout U.S. history, the ruling classes have worked to divide the multinational U.S. working class in order to maintain the capitalist social order. As a result, not only are workers exploited in their jobs, some face special oppressions, as Black people do in the U.S.

Black workers are oppressed by a system of white supremacy which developed alongside American capitalism, and led to its rapid development through the extraction of super profits from enslaved Black labor. The construction of a system of white supremacy was an intentional creation of the white capitalist ruling class in order to stratify all of the laboring peoples creating "races" with the "white race" being at the top of the racial hierarchy. Black people were legally constructed as "three-fifths" of a person and thus struggled fundamentally for their recognition as human beings. Due to the history of American capitalism, and the role that Black people have played in its development, Black liberation is one of the sharpest class struggles under capitalism: it is a detonating factor because of the class composition of the Black nation, which makes it feared by the ruling class and promising for the people's struggle.

Black revolutionary, Eugene Puryear, writing in the midst of the historic anti-racist rebellion that mobilized 35 million Americans in the wake of the murder of George Floyd, explains:

The oppression of Black America is so central to the country that the struggle for Black Liberation has often acted as a detonator, so to speak, setting off broader social struggles throughout the system. In today's volatile mix, the charges now rigged to blow may be too difficult for capitalism to withstand.[4]

The Black working class is a powder keg for revolution and the ruling classes know it. This is why they attempt to erase Black history and repress the Black struggle through mass incarceration, racist police terror, political repression, and even accommodation. This is why they go to such lengths to create illusions of Black inclusion by enabling a "Black" capitalism tied to white monopoly capital by a thousand and one threads. By denying that Black struggle is class struggle, the ruling class promotes a politics of inclusion that simultaneously denies Black self-determination *and* the democratic integration of Black people.

When we approach Black struggle as the struggle of an entire nation of people for self-determination, our class analysis is sharpened and our unity is strengthened. The struggles of Black and other oppressed peoples are struggles for liberation from capitalist society, not an attempt to seek peace or integration with capitalist society.

---

4   Puryear, Eugene. (2020). "From Rebellion to Revolution," *Liberation News*, June 29. Available online at: https://www.liberationnews.org/from-rebellion-to-revolution/.

The U.S. Working Class Today: A Material Basis for Multinational Unity

Since the end of the period of Reconstruction, U.S. capitalism has grown into imperialism, the highest stage of capitalism. In our current period, the imperialists impose their rule by indirect means using finance capital to strangulate nations and economies of the world into subservience. In the era of imperialism, of capitalism's general decline, the role of the Black working class in the "belly of the beast" has been drawn into sharper contradiction and the historic anti-racist rebellions of 2020 demonstrate yet again the vanguard role of Black workers in leading the multinational working class against its common enemy: capitalist-imperialism.

The technological revolution that began in the 1970s—having continued to this day—has since fundamentally changed the social composition of the U.S. working class, contributing to the possibilities of unity and the building of a revolutionary movement that truly unites all of those who are at the bottom of class society. In the U.S., this means uniting the 140 million poor or near poor working class people, of all nationalities but primarily and increasingly Black, Latino, and Native into a single, united class struggle. The horizon for class struggle must be the multinational working class, in its full diversity, against the multinational ruling class, anchored by white monopoly capital. The mad dash for profits and super-profits and the development of the bourgeoisie has broadened the material basis for working class unity around a socialist program led by a single, multinational communist party.

The historic anti-racist rebellions of 2020 in the throes of a deadly global pandemic evinced a picture of the revolution to come. Even the bourgeois mouthpiece, the *New York Times* admitted that the 2020 rebellions demonstrated a multinational character and broad geographic spread for the protests.

Across the United States, there have been more than 4,700 demonstrations, or an average of 140 per day, since the first protests began in Minneapolis on May 26, according to a *Times* analysis. Turnout has ranged from dozens to tens of thousands in about 2,500 small towns and large cities. More than 40 percent of counties in the United States—

at least 1,360—have had a protest. Unlike with past Black Lives Matter protests, nearly 95 percent of counties that had a protest recently are majority white, and nearly three-quarters of the counties are more than 75 percent white.[5]

The fractures within U.S. capitalism's political superstructure are deepening and the popularity of socialist politics mounts, yet we are not out of the waters just yet. As the events of January 6th, 2021 demonstrated to many Americans, we could quite easily have outright fascist rule in this country.

It is now objectively possible to build a unified workers' movement with a multinational leadership. In fact, the very real opportunity of political leadership by the historically most oppressed sectors puts the working class today in a stronger position to struggle for power. Fighting racism and national oppression has to find its way into the forefront of every struggle under capitalism—and for a proletarian party, this is the only way real unity between white workers and Black, Latino and other oppressed nations will be forged. As Hubert Harrison reminded the Socialist Party, so, too, must we constantly remind ourselves that: "We are not a white man's party or a [B]lack man's party, but the party of the working class. And the historic mission of the Socialist movement is to unite the workers of the world."[6]

---

5   Buchanan, Larry, Quoctrung Bui, and Jugal K. Patel. (2020). "Black Lives Matter May Be the Largest Movement in U.S. History," *New York Times*, July 3. Available online at: https://www.nytimes.com/interactive/2020/07/03/us/george-floyd-protests-crowd-size.html

6   Harrison, Hubert. (2001). "The Duty of Socialist Party," in the *Hubert Harrison Reader*, Jeffery B. Perry, ed. (Middletown, CT, Wesleyan Press).

SECTION 2
Arts & Culture

CHAPTER 3
SIN FRONTERAS: DISPATCHES FROM MEXICO CITY

David A. Romero

DAVID A. ROMERO is a Mexican-American spoken word artist from Diamond Bar, CA. Romero is the author of *My Name Is Romero* (FlowerSong Press), a book reviewed by Gustavo Arellano (¡Ask a Mexican!), Curtis Marez *(University Babylon)*, and founding member of Ozomatli, Ulises Bella. Romero has received honorariums from over seventy-five colleges and universities in thirty-four different states in the USA and has performed live in Mexico, Italy, and France. Romero's work has been published in literary magazines in the United States, Mexico, England, Scotland, and Canada. Romero has opened for Latin Grammy-winning bands Ozomatli and La Santa Cecilia. Romero's work has been published in anthologies alongside poets laureate Joy Harjo, Lawrence Ferlinghetti, Luis J. Rodriguez, Jack Hirschman, and Tongo Eisen-Martin. Romero has won the Uptown Slam at the historic Green Mill in Chicago; the birthplace of slam poetry. Romero's poetry deals with family, identity, social justice issues, and Latinx culture.

All photos of the event, included in this article, were captured by Carmen Harumi V. Leos.

November 15-19, 2022

A DELEGATION OF CHICANO POETS, artists, and intellectuals flew to Mexico City for five events over the course of four days across the city.

It all began with a series of emails and social media messages flying across the Mexico-United States border. One poet, Matt Sedillo, Literary Director of the Mexican Cultural Institute of Los Angeles, and one academic, Alfonso Vázquez, founder of the Chicanxs Sin Fronteras project in Mexico City, first made their acquaintance virtually, and eventually, made plans together to bring a delegation from the U.S. to Mexico.

"In my first conversation with Alfonso, I told him I had spoken all over the world, that I had even spoken at Cambridge. While that was a huge honor, my real dream was UNAM," said Sedillo of those early exchanges.

A professor at FES Acatlán (UNAM) and the author of a history of Chicano cinema and media representation in Spanish, *Chicano* (University of Guanajuato, 2018), Vázquez knew he could make Sedillo's dream a reality.

"There is a great reception and interest in Chicano culture in Mexico." Said Vázquez in an interview with Nancy Cázares, of *La Izquierda Diario*.

Alongside his partner Abril Zaragoza, Vázquez has created Chicanxs Sin Fronteras to "disseminate and bring young people and the general public closer to Chicano culture beyond the stereotypes that have been imposed on the Mexican who lives in the United States."

Sedillo and Vázquez developed a four-day literary and arts series of events across Mexico City with the coordination of the Mexican Cultural Institute of Los Angeles and Chicanxs Sin Fronteras, along with the latter organization's frequent collaborators: Tianguis Literario CDMX (a collective led by young poet Yasmín Alfaro) and Gorrión Editorial (a publishing house run by poet and professor Abraham Peralta Vélez)—collectively entitled: *Desfronterizxs. Homenaje a la escritora Gloria Anzaldúa. Encuentro de poesía chicana.*

Sedillo's delegation flying in from the U.S., a mix of those born in the U.S. and in Mexico, was a "dream team" that included the Director of the Mexican Cultural Institute of Los Angeles, the muralist Jose Antonio Aguirre, poets and professors Norma Elia Cantú and Gabriella Gutiérrez y Muhs (both of whom knew the series' figure of homage, Gloria E. Anzaldúa, personally), community activist and author of *Always Running: La Vida Loca, Gang Days in L.A.* (Atria, 2005), Luis J. Rodriguez; the sociologist and organizer of delegations to Cuba, Jose Prado; the art curator and organizer of events at El Camino College in Los Angeles, Dulce Stein; and the author of *My Name Is Romero* (FlowerSong Press, 2020)—and writer of this article—myself, David A. Romero.

Norma Elia Cantú, along with sharing her poetry, carried the special honor of giving a multimedia presentation on Anzaldúa's life, work, and philosophy. Cantú's own reputation, as the recipient of over a dozen awards and the author of dozens of books, including *Canícula: Snapshots of a Girlhood en la Frontera* (University of New Mexico Press, 1997), preceded her in CDMX. Many of the professors and students in attendance were excited to meet her in person.

The delegation from the U.S. presented from November 15-19, 2022 in locations as varied as the universities FES Acatlán (UNAM), La Casa de la Universidad de California en México (UC system), the high school CCH Naucalpan (UNAM), the activist café La Resistencia, and arts center Gimnasio de arte y cultura in Roma (formerly the home of the Partido Popular Socialista).

At FES Acatlán, La Casa de la Universidad de California en México, and CCH Naucalpan, the delegation from the U.S. presented with introductions from Vázquez and organizers at their respective campuses: María del Consuelo Santamaría Aguirre, Jeohvan Jedidian Silva Sánchez, Keshava R. Quintanar Cano, Eva Daniela Sandoval Espejo, and Efraín Refugio Lugo.

At La Resistencia and Gimnasio de arte y cultura, the delegation was joined by the Mexican poets, writers, and performers: Pita Ochoa, Cynthia Franco, Sara Raca, Abraham Peralta Vélez, Yasmin Alfaro, Bajo Palabra, Rubikon, Omar Jasso, Lumen Eros Vita, Imperio Soul, and DJ Paolo Guerrero, all of whom were excited to share their work alongside the delegation and to represent their country.

The delegation from the U.S. was embraced in all places by their Mexican hosts, who welcomed them into their institutions, presented them with certificates of thanks, took photos with them and purchased their books, escorted them on trips throughout the city to visit historic places of interest, and for many members, even welcomed them into their own homes and the homes of their extended families.

Outside of the events, the trip held special meaning for members of the delegation. For Jose Antonio Aguirre, who holds dual citizenship and makes frequent trips to his homeland, the trip to Mexico City was nevertheless an opportunity to meet up with his daughter and to reconnect with an old friend. For Luis J. Rodriguez and Dulce Stein, it was an opportunity to connect with family members they had never met. In the case of Rodriguez, those family members were the children of his aunt Chucha, the namesake of his cultural center in Sylmar, Tia Chucha's, which has served its community for over twenty years.

For Sedillo, the author of *Mowing Leaves of Grass* (FlowerSong Press, 2019), the trip to Mexico City had a less direct, but still profound cultural and spiritual meaning: "It's every Chicano's dream to be welcomed back home—to Tenochtitlan."

The Historical Significance of the Chicano Delegation to Mexico City

Gloria Anzaldúa traveled to Mexico City to teach a graduate seminar "La Identidad Estadounidense" at UNAM's main campus in 2013. A handful of other noted writers of Mexican descent born in the U.S., including Sandra Cisneros and Roberto Tejada, have both lived in the metropolis on and off for decades and have given readings in the city, sometimes inviting their contemporaries from the U.S. to join them.

However, there is no bridge that has been regularly maintained, neither by universities nor cultural centers in Mexico City, to bring in Chicano writers and poets to share their work and build a connection between the communities in earnest.

For over a century, the populations have been separated: by border, by language, by history, by culture. It may have seemed unlikely, if not impossible, for the Chicano and Chilango to come together and to build together.

In the U.S., Chicanos, whether those with longstanding ties to the borderlands or the children of immigrants, are often treated as second-class citizens, lumped into a category known as "minority," or (more generously) as "people of color," subject to microaggressions, labor exploitation, criminalization, and violence. Ours is a history of struggle and poverty. Of the antagonism between assimilation and resistance. Of constantly being uncertain of our futures and of who we are. Of being *ni aquí ni allá*. We are a people often defined by what we are not.

The Mexicans of Mexico City, the Chilangos, can seem to be the opposite, as people who are certain, who are defined, who are. They are the majority population. The normal. The normative. The unquestioned. They live in their capital, a world city, cosmopolitan and international in their tastes. Everywhere, they pull from the character of their nation, producing a synthesis, one that may vary from neighborhood, but that is proud. That is Mexican. They are fluent in Spanish, because prima facie, that is their language. Everywhere in CDMX, there is a tie to both the recent and ancient past. They live in Tenochtitlan; the ruins of Templo Mayor within arm's reach and mere feet away from the Zócalo and the National Palace. Monuments to their heroes abound in bust and sculpture—and their heroes all look like them.

For a time, it could seem that we, the Chicano and the Chilango, could not be more different. What sense would the tales of uncertainty and second-class citizenship make to a Chilango? How could the Chicano, who directly or indirectly benefits from U.S. imperialism, respond to accusations that they are implicit in the modern-day gentrification and subjugation of their motherland?

And yet, culture connects us: music, art, film, literature. As in Japan and Thailand, Chicano culture has saturated Mexico City. The cholo is cool. Chicano is cool. Chicano es chido. But, unlike in Japan and Thailand where the connection is deeply felt, but somewhat cosmetic, the Chilangos know that, although divided, although different, the Chicano and Chilango share the same blood. We are the same people.

"The borders aren't real. They're not like the rivers or mountains. They weren't made by God. They were made by man. This land is one. All of the Americas are our community." Luis J. Rodriguez, the former poet laureate of Los Angeles, said, passionately, to the students at FES Acatlán.

During a short presentation at CCH Naucalpan, Jose Antonio Aguirre described himself, humorously, "I am from Ciudad de México. I am a Chilango. But I have also lived in the United States for a long time, and am influenced by the Chicanos. So, I call myself a Chicalango."

In one of the most powerful moments of the event series, Gabriella Gutiérrez y Muhs, the author of *Presumed Incompetent: The Intersections of Race and Class for Women in Academia* (Utah State University Press, 2012) , asked the over one hundred in attendance at CCH Naucalpan for a show of hands. "How many of you have family in the United States?" Almost everyone in the audience raised their hands. She added, speaking of Chicanos in Mexico, "This is our country, too."

Alfonso Vázquez, a Chilango with family in California, knows this isn't an isolated phenomenon, "Many of our families, many states of the Republic have a great tradition around to migration, they are migrant states: Michoacán, Jalisco, Guanajuato, Zacatecas, are states with a great tradition. There are also many migrants in Mexico City, it is a place from where many people leave for other states, and to the United States, of course."

Vázquez partnered with CCH Naucalpan and Gorrión Editorial to collect work from the writers of the delegation from the U.S. into a special collection entitled, *Ellos son nosotros* (*They are us*), with translations of works in English into Spanish and art by Jose Antonio Aguirre. The message from the Chilangos to the Chicanos could not be clearer.

A Bridge that Goes Both Ways

"We thank you. For creating a bridge into Mexico." Matt Sedillo said, to close out his set at Gimnasio de arte y cultura, wiping sweat off his brow and addressing the crowd of Mexican organizers and artists present. "I recognize a bridge goes both ways. It's not just for us to come here. But for us [Chicanos], to host you [in the United States]."

The words of Anzaldúa ring, "*Caminante, no hay puentes, se hace puentes al andar.*"

For Sedillo, who has sailed to the island of Elba, taken trains to Paris, flown to Ravenna to receive the Dante's Laurel, and likewise, traveled to Cuba, England, Mexico, and Canada, the task of continuing to work with Vázquez to build such a bridge between Mexico and Los Angeles is not merely a challenge as the Literary Director of the Mexican Cultural Institute of Los Angeles, it's in his job description, and it is the greatest opportunity he can imagine.

CHAPTER 4
ANTI-ABLEIST TEACHING STRATEGIES AND DISABILITY LIFE PHOTOGRAPHY

Sarah Pfohl

SARAH PFOHL is a dis/abled, chronically ill artist and teacher. She makes work about the value, power, and complexity of: a rural New York hill, the disabled body, and classroom teaching. Sarah serves as Assistant Professor of Photography and Art Education Coordinator in the Department of Art & Design at the University of Indianapolis. She lives in Indianapolis and Hubbardsville, NY. Sarah's work has been exhibited and published nationally and internationally. Her photographs have been included in group exhibitions at SF Camerawork (San Francisco), Filter Space (Chicago), The Reference (Seoul), Polygon Gallery (Vancouver), and theprintspace gallery (London). Sarah has participated in publications issued by Halfmoon Projects (Chicago), Oranbeg Press (Brooklyn), Soft Lightning (Brooklyn), Nightbird Zine (NY), Quiet Pages Press (PA), Goldenrod Editions (NY), Don't Smile (FL), Funny Looking Dog Quarterly (Chicago), and Pine Island Press (Portland, OR).

I'M A PROUDLY DIS/ABLED, chronically ill artist and teacher and about 15 years ago, as a graduate student studying education, I came into contact with ideas from disability liberation that completely turned inside out my thinking about myself as a sick person. Over time, these ideas have become foundational to me as both an artist and a teacher. I'll share a few of those ideas with you, offer some ways you might bring them into your own work with people (in teaching or beyond), if you don't already, and then talk about the photographic work I've been making inspired by the anti-ableist movement that is disability liberation. I'll move in a couple of different directions—teaching, theory, identity, and artistic work. In my body-mind, life, and work, it's all intertwined.

A few final contextualizing notes by way of introduction. First, notes on language. In this talk, I'll refer to *ableism*, which is oppression based on real or perceived aspects of a person or group's ability. The language I'll use throughout this talk is specific and intentional, it may sometimes meet you as surprising. Next, I'll draw ideas from lots of different arenas of thinking and action including disability studies, disability rights, and disability justice. This talk will provide a really quick, condensed introduction to a few pieces of a huge, rich terrain. I'm skating across the surface, please check out the resource guide for more information, if you're so inclined, or reach out, I'm happy to chat further.

I'm one person among so many within the disability community. Data estimate that one in four U.S. adults under the age of 65 manages a diagnosis. In other words, the disability community is huge, there are almost certainly disabled people in your midst, whether you realize it or not. The community encompasses billions of people worldwide. I'll speak here through the lens of my own experiences and on behalf of myself, not on behalf of an entire group of incredibly diverse people.

Finally, a "why should you care?" note. Taken as a whole, the concepts I offer here mean to invite, increase, and normalize meaningful participation in our world from a huge group of individuals positioned as less than, a huge group of individuals whose separation from the non-disabled world is deeply rationalized, dominantly framed as humane, and in many cases currently legal. Disabled people deserve humane treatment and full participation and have incredibly valuable perspectives and knowledge to contribute to our world.

Anti-Ableist Teaching Strategies

First, I'll cover three concepts in contemporary disability liberation that might be of use in teaching and learning contexts and beyond. I'll define each one, or, in one case, a paired set, and then talk a little bit about practical implications.

I'll talk first about the intertwined concepts of the medical model of disability and the social model of disability.

The medical model and social model construct disability in two diametrically opposed ways; in particular, they locate the origins of disability in two very different places. Taken together, the medical and social models can point toward ways in which contexts disable people.

The image of the medical model centers around a (frowning) person using a mobility assistive device (e.g., crutch) and a prosthetic next to a step. The problem is clearly the person's mobility; their body and the way it moves. The image of the social model centers around a person using a similar device to move, like a wheelchair, who is confronted with steep steps. The problem is not the person but the organization of society. Within the medical model perspective, we see disability defined as an *impairment*—through this, it is referred to in deficit-centric, negative terms. This positioning of disability as a limitation, a disorder, or a disadvantage is a key characteristic of the medical model. Additionally in the medical model perspective, disability is defined as a condition rooted within an individual, it's a problem, located first and foremost within a person. By extension, the diagnosed person becomes the problem, especially if they can't be "fixed."

The social model perspective provides a counterpoint arguing that disability is not always and only located within the individual, rather it is socially agreed upon and produced out of the interaction between people and the world around them. Within the context of the social model of disability, inflexible, rigid, beliefs, attitudes, and physical structures produce what we call disability through the pathological unwillingness of those forces to shift or change such that they may accommodate a wider range of human diversity.

The social model doesn't position the disabled person as a problem or as in need of fixing. Rather, it provides a perspective that normalizes human difference as a fact of human life, rather than pathologizing certain ways of being in favor of upholding existing, oftentimes-ableist social norms.

In the dominant culture, the medical model is normative—you probably have extensive experience with it just by being alive in the world—while the social model of disability reframes thinking and conversations about ability fundamentally. For the purposes of teaching, the paired models provide a number of possibly useful implications:

1. Remember that there are a growing number of disabled people who view disability as a part of their identity that connects them

to a rich, important, diverse culture with an exciting history and future. Disability pride is a real thing.

2. Expect diversity in conceptualizing your teaching. Folks interested in realizing more ability-inclusive teaching moves might check out the Universal Design for Learning framework for suggestions. UDL encourages educators to provide multiple pathways into content engagement alongside multiple means of content representation and learning expression. Within a teaching context, flexibility can be a powerful anti-ableist teaching move.

3. Be thoughtful about the elements of your teaching practice designed to socialize students into an existing normative framework. If you are socializing students toward something, what is the lineage behind that something? I bring this up because when I've led PD on these topics previously, one of the most common pieces of pushback I get is—but it's my job to socialize my students even if that's ability-exclusive. Some teachers resist the social model lens because part of their mission is conforming their students to productivity relative to the existing social order. You might be mindful of this, as it can be ability-exclusive given the intense ableism present in our existing social order.

A few critical notes here:

1. The social model of disability, when present in public discourse, is poorly understood and often completely misconstrued. I strongly encourage you not to Google it, because the results bear little relation to the actuality of the concept.

2. The social model doesn't argue against medical intervention. It is not saying that one should stop going to the doctor or that medical support is a bad thing. It does argue that disability-related expertise can be located in many places, within and beyond medical practitioners.

3. Finally, the social model doesn't argue that disabled people must embrace, love, and be happy about being disabled. It does challenge the idea that disability is always and only a negative thing, but doesn't prescribe the feelings disabled people "should" have about themselves.

The next concept I wanted to bring into the room is much narrower in scope—I wanted to talk about presuming competence as a mindset and lens. I first encountered this concept in Kathleen Collins' great book *Ability Profiling and School Failure: One Child's Struggle to Be Seen as Competent*.

The simple yet revolutionary argument embedded within presuming competence is that disabled people have capacity. Disabled people are often always and only framed around what they can't do, especially educationally, and the list of can't dos becomes the center column of that individual's identity for others. We see this happen educationally especially when the terms of someone's accommodation rub up against the teaching norms already in place in a particular instructor's teaching and learning context/teaching practice. Years ago, I worked with an art history professor who very emphatically didn't allow students to have screens of any kind in their classes but received, during the first week of school, an accommodation letter from a student indicating that they required the use of a laptop for note-taking during class meetings. Of course, an ADA accommodation is a legally-binding document, and violating the terms of an accommodation is a violation of the student's federally-mandated civil rights under the ADA. The student became "the student who can't write their own notes by hand" and instead of finding a creative solution, the professor pushed the student out of the class. They told the student to either stop using the screen or sit in the back of the classroom so that they didn't "distract" their peers with the screen. The student dropped the class in response.

Disabled people can do a lot of things! We carry so much capacity. Finding creative ways to align existing circumstances with an individual's existing capacities to in turn promote more full participation can produce more ability-based inclusion for all. An argument for teaching from disability liberation is to keep the learning goals the same but increase the pathways toward them. A couple years ago I worked with a sculpture professor who had a project that included chop saw use. He knew several incoming students would not be able to use the chop saw as it was installed in the wood shop. In conversation, it turned out that the primary project learning goal was centered around creating a modular object, so in that particular case increasing the number of materials with which students could work, allowing students to work with both wood and paper, increased accessibility while maintaining the project objectives.

The last concept that I want to talk about is language associated with disability. Here the literature has a couple of different suggestions. The first suggestion has to do with ability-related identifiers people use. Here's a list of preferred ability identifiers of some of my friends: disabled, dis/abled, disabled, sick, crip, mad, neurodivergent, chronically ill, ability non-normative, disabled person, person with a disability, physically ill, mentally ill, sick

Which ones are right? There are no monolithically correct identifiers that I know of at this time.

Don't most of these words mean the same thing? No, they don't. Disability as an identity and cultural category is incredibly diverse; one person's relationship to a particular identifier may be totally different from another person's relationship to the same word.

Here's what I can offer: People's identifiers are highly specific and personal, use the language offered by individuals as they offer it. In the same way that you wouldn't correct a student on the spelling of their name or pronoun use, don't correct someone's ability-related identifiers—accept what they tell you. Different identifiers do connect to different movements and spheres of thinking within disability liberation. Assume people use the language with which they identify themselves intentionally and honor it.

In my own case, I use dis/abled and chronically ill. I use the word disabled to name the social conditions under which I live my life. What I mean by that is that I live in a world that constantly, tens of times each day, reminds me that I don't belong here and I should normalize or get out because the diversity I embody isn't important.

I write dis/abled with a backslash between dis and abled to connect myself explicitly back to disability studies. Dis/abled is how some folks in disability studies write disabled to underscore the socially constructed nature of disability at a formal, linguistic level and that resonates for me, so I use it. Disability studies is also where I first encountered ideas that fundamentally reframed my thinking about ability and illness, so my use of a term anchored there as an identifier does honor others' works and points toward my affiliations.

I say 'chronically ill' to hold up and foreground my biological reality as a person engaged in the constant labor and care associated with managing multiple, incurable diagnoses.

And all of these will grow and change as the movement grows and changes, which is a beautiful thing.

Second, relative to disability-related language I wanted to be sure to identify the distinction between person-first and identity-first language. Many folks have heard of person-first language as it pertains to ability. To summarize, the idea is that one says "individual with a disability" or "person with [insert diagnosis]" foregrounding the person first and ability status second, rather than the inverse—foregrounding the ability status first and the person second. Folks who ascribe to person-first linguistic patterns argue that by naming first the individual, the individual becomes less defined by their ability status.

Identity-first language turns that around and argues that linguistically foregrounding ability-related identity by saying "disabled person" promotes disability pride and de-stigmatizes oftentimes negative preconceptions of the word disabled. Some proponents of identity-first language also argue that in using that language pattern they name disabled people's life experiences as they more truly are—an ableist world reminds disabled people that they do not belong. A common argument against person-first language from a disabled person is, "I'll use person-first language when I start getting treated like a person." As you may have noticed, I'm using identity-first language throughout this presentation.

For a long time, person-first language (person with a disability) was far more common and that linguistic norm is very present in many fields, especially medical and educational spheres. It isn't a bad approach, especially if you're non-disabled and talking about disability or you find yourself in the position of having to choose one or the other. In those moments, person-first works great.

However, if you encounter someone, like a student, who is disabled and uses identity-first language, honor that. Again, use the identifiers someone supplies you and assume the identifiers used are used intentionally. Resist the urge to teach a disabled person who identifies as a disabled person about person-first language.

The final perspective from the intersections between language and ability I wanted to offer to this space is an invitation to use and model anti-ableist language.

Ableist slurs are quite common and often used unintentionally. They might emerge as language patterns that position a diagnosis category or way of being in general in a negative light or from a deficit standpoint. A few examples and how they would be corrected:

1. I was engaged in a *blind* struggle to move forward—I was engaged in a *careless* struggle to move forward.
2. He's *stuck* in a wheelchair—He *uses* a wheelchair.
3. That's a *lame* excuse—That's an *inadequate* excuse.

It seems subtle, but it's a big deal. I find that more and more of my students know this content and read the world around them, looking for mentors and allyship, informed by the subtle hints provided by the gatekeepers in their lives. Lots of disabled young people in higher education don't and won't disclose but need help and actively decreasing ableist slur use helps vulnerable students find folks who can provide critical support. Again, the tip of a huge iceberg but a brief outline of ideas I've come into contact with that have been useful to me as a teacher.

As I mentioned, statistically one in four U.S. adults under the age of 65 fall into the category of disabled. This would mean, if, for example, you're a teacher in higher education, that in a class of 20 students, you should statistically receive five accommodation letters. Of course, there are many reasons people don't self-identify formally through disability services. I share these numbers to underscore that ability-related non-normativity may be far more present in the spaces within which you move than you realize. These ideas, aimed at promoting the humanity and humane treatment of people historically treated terribly can have a big impact even if you think they might not pertain to you.

Imaging What's Wrong With Me

I'll shift now to the artistic work I've been making precipitated by the ideas I just shared and start with some facts about my body.

The primary biological diagnosis with which I was born is currently called osteogenesis imperfecta, abbreviated as OI. As a diagnosis category, OI is characterized by the OI Foundation, the primary US-based advocacy body associated with it, as "complicated, variable, and rare" in appearance. Statistically, worldwide, around 1 in every 15,000-20,000 people lives with osteogenesis imperfecta. Within the context of my own life, I've never knowingly met in person someone else with OI.

With OI, which is incurable, I have less of a particular protein in my body than deemed medically normal and within that, the smaller amount of that protein I do have is designated, in medical terms, as "qualitatively abnormal," which is one of the many fun things I get to hear medical professionals I've just met call me—"qualitatively abnormal."

More specifically, parts of my body—my bones, heart, lungs, eyes, and ears—work differently than most other people's. My bones break, sometimes for little or no discernible reason. I've broken bones in my legs, arms, hands, feet, fingers, and toes, I've fractured my pelvis, my skull, and both clavicles. I can have trouble with the mechanics of my body; my ability to walk ebbs and flows.

I also manage now OI's offshoots and degenerative progressions, as a diagnosis it proliferates over time. I manage Deaf gain (referred to as hearing loss in hearing culture), early-onset osteoporosis, anxiety, and depression. So that's a brief description of the nature of my body-mind from a medicalized, biological, diagnosis-label perspective.

I share this not in an attempt to evoke sympathy or pity, but to outline what counts as normal within the context of my own experience. As a site, my body requires constant management and care. I share information also to cure any deniers—I don't usually read as disabled and chronically ill, it's common for people to question me on that, so specifics and disclosing can help build my credibility.

As a dis/abled, chronically ill artist coming into contact with ideas from disability liberation, I started to wonder what implications they might have for my artistic work. As I worked to shift my consciousness away from medical model thinking and toward social model interpretations of the world around me, I began to notice and become more critical of the negative representational tropes associated with illness and disability that permeated the world around me. Experiences of disability are incredibly diverse but, due to ableism, the visual language commonly associated with disability was narrow and unimaginative.

As I started to photograph toward my own representation of disability, I wanted to visually push back against these norms. A question I started to chew on often was, "Can I make a representation of disability that feels true to my lived experience, that doesn't include the body, and that goes beyond the common, deficit-centric narrative?"

I looked around for some inspiration. I started to notice also that the representations of disability that presented the most complex, nuanced portraits of diagnosis management and ability non-normative life were first-person. By "first-person" I mean they were crafted by an individual with first-hand experience in diagnosis management. I had been reading within the field of disability life writing, an approach to writing that argues for the value of diverse narratives about disability written by disabled people, and started to look for examples of disability life photography.

Through the lens of the social model of disability, a disabled person is positioned as the primary expert on their own life and body-mind. A disabled person is, through the social model lens, a knowledgeable authority on what it is to be sick. This social model perspective overturns dominant medical model thinking which locates disability-related expertise in basically anyone except the disabled individual. For example, it's quite common for a medical professional's perspective on an illness they have never experienced to be held in higher regard than the perspective of an individual in medical care experiencing that particular illness; an insidious norm that extends historical positioning of the disabled person as helpless and wholly reliant when in reality, of course, the person who knows the most about a particular body is the one living within it.

Within photography, I came into contact with work by artists like Jaklin Romine, Megan Bent, Sara J. Winston, and Frances Bukovsky. I gained so much inspiration from this work, and it really gave me the steam and permission I needed to believe first-person ability-related representations were both critical and far more rare than ideal.

With a bit of visual footing, I moved forward. As a diagnosis management strategy, I am prescribed daily walks. I walk often in a forested, public park near my home in Indianapolis and I began to take my camera with me and photograph botanical forms during my walk.

I work very intuitively and started to photograph in the forest without any particular ambition for the images in mind. Strategically, I did want to photograph while walking to combine two necessary tasks in my life—these prescribed walks, as required by my doctor, and producing artistic work, as required by my job and spirit.

Being disabled and chronically ill, my time is structured toward preserving my life in a very specific, calculated way. I spend a lot of time on diagnosis management and care each day, stewarding my body, and then far more time dealing with the MIC, the medical industrial complex—spending my precious time engaged in tasks like the following: on the phone with healthcare providers, driving to appointments, engaged in appointments, on the phone with co-pay programs and my health insurance, trying to recover emotionally from the ups and downs of medical news and receiving surprise medical bills to the tune of thousands of dollars.

Folding diagnosis management and making together, pairing two things I had to do, helped me feel more in control of my time and body. I also wanted to take a demand from and limitation of my diagnosed body, its need for these walks, and reframe it as a generative space by building photographing into the ritual practice of care rooted in these walks.

As I reviewed the work I made in the park, I found myself most drawn to the blurry, indistinct backgrounds in the images and I began to lean into that. Again and again, as I looked through the photographs, paying closer attention to the blurred-out components over the sharp ones, the phrase, "That looks like me." popped unbidden into my mind. Over time, the phrase grew into a conviction and I've found that for me, one of the most important parts of growing into an artist has been learning to take seriously and interrogate the weird, unexplainable truths my body-mind unbidden offers.

As I investigated my identification with blurry botanical forms, I realized my photographs contained visual continuities with the medical imagining I encountered in my daily life. They looked like microscopic versions of medical evidence related to my diagnoses.

They looked like x-ray enlargements, the thready-ness of bone, the haziness of tissue.

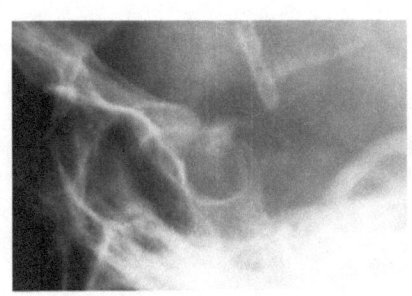

Credit: Craniopharyngioma. Wellcome Collection. Attribution 4.0 International (CC BY 4.0).

Over the course of my life as a multiply-diagnosed person, I have likely been medically and diagnostically-imaged more than I have been photographed for memory's sake. Put another way, I think there are probably more representations of me in the form of diagnostic evidence like x-rays than there are pictures of me traveling, with friends, at parties, etc. This isn't to say I don't go out, it is to underline that my experience as a patient in medical settings is extensive and life-long.

Image 1. *Osteogenesis imperfecta model no. 45.*

I found tremendous power in creating my own weird version of diagnostic-ish imagery. I can't underline that enough. After years as subject to medicalized imaging practices, for the first time, I was the person making the x-ray, taking the scan, in effect pressing the shutter release from within my radiation-protected bubble rather than the individual lying prone and covered with lead on a cold plastic table while a device circled my body as it emitted a series of beeps.

Visually, I think of the work as messy, a resolved but wild tangle that flickers between clarity and ambiguity. Born into a body that carries multiple non-visible diagnoses, my external appearance and my internal reality rarely coincide, especially within the world of the general public imagination. In other words, I don't look like one of the most foundational aspects of who and what I am, I pass for fine but am pretty sick, and that tends to trip people up. I continued to think about that phrase, "That looks like me," and realized the flora I trained my lens toward and then intentionally rendered out through the camera as disorienting, messy thickets punctuated by moments of clarity aligned with the illegibility foundational to my lived experience of non-visible illness.

On one hand, I can say my visible appearance misdirects, a symbol for lived experiences I have never known and will never know. My external body feels like a costume that doesn't fit or a deception. On the other hand, common ideas of what disability looks like bear very little relationship to the hugely diverse ways in which disability actually presents. Through this, I become clear in flashes.

Being read and socially positioned as non-disabled is, of course, at times a privilege but in some circumstances can be incredibly dangerous. My life has been put in danger many times because people assumed I wasn't sick and ascribed abilities to me I didn't have or expected performance from me I could not provide. In these moments of illegibility, my choice is disclosure or danger.

Image 2. *Osteogenesis imperfecta model no. 97.*

Additionally, I can't tell you how many times I've disclosed in an attempt to pull myself out of danger but have been denied (literally told things like "that's not possible," "no, you don't") because I don't live up

Image 3. *Osteogenesis imperfecta model no. 76*

to someone else's version of what a disabled person looks like. It's this strange struggle to be seen and I found image-making processes that I could use to render visually these feelings. The anti-ableist teaching implications here are to two-fold: 1) trust what people tell you about their circumstances, even if they don't/can't provide medical documentation, and 2) don't forget that interior and exterior circumstances don't always align.

I started to think of the work as my body without my body, as non-traditional self-portraits. A piece of useful context here is that I grew up in rural New York, two miles outside of a village of about 650 people. I spent my first 18 years surrounded by far more plants and trees than people and, this isn't a joke, my first best friends were the wild grasses and greenery around my parents' house. That, within the context of this particular body of work, I've located botanical forms as a stand-in for my innermost physical realities and psychological experiences align with the deep flora connections I witnessed and cultivated within the rural culture I know best.

I don't prescribe to the medical model idea of disability as a monolithically bad thing. Like many folks in the disability liberation community, I wouldn't take a cure if I were offered one, and I locate some of the aspects of my personality that have become the most valuable to me as originating in and inseparable from my lived experiences as a disabled person. My incurable body is my superpower and in spite of powerful, oftentimes-eugenic societal messages to the contrary it has never served me to believe I'm less-than, that there's something "wrong with me" because of the diagnoses I manage. I wanted to make a representation of disability that contained moments of beauty to honor the power and value of disability as I know it.

Image 3. *Osteogenesis imperfecta model no. 5.*

The last framing note I'll share relative to this ongoing work—many disabled, chronically ill people maintain a dossier of critical medical information. This dossier might include hundreds of pages of content like care information and instructions, health insurance documents (if one has health insurance), diagnoses, or emergency information. My dossier is a 3-inch, blue, 3-ring binder that I take with me to medical facilities to prove myself and direct my care, especially in emergency situations. Because the primary diagnosis I manage is rare and medical professionals are taught that common diagnoses are common (when you hear hooves, think *horses*, not *zebras*) I often have to tell the people taking care of me what to do. Sometimes, I am the first person with OI a medical professional with whom I'm working has ever met *in person*.

Taken together the images in this ongoing project operate as a slant dossier. They are the models of my lived experiences of rare, non-visible diagnoses. They are evidence of my internal genetic reality as I imagine it models my social experiences of sickness in a deeply ableist world. Sometimes I wonder what would happen if I could take my pictures to a medical professional and be like, "Here, this is my version of what's wrong with me. Diagnose this." Finally—I will just mention quickly—my idea right now is for the project to include 206 individual images in its final form, one for each bone in most adult human bodies.

ANTI-ABLEIST TEACHING STRATEGIES 53

Image 4. *Osteogenesis imperfecta model no. 55.*

A Resource Guide

SOME VERY GOOD BOOKS

Rethinking disability: A disability studies approach to inclusive practices, Jan W. Valle and David J. Connor, 2019 (2nd ed.), Routledge (disability studies)

Any text by Eli Clare. A great starting point: *Brilliant imperfection: Grappling with cure*, Eli Clare, 2017, Duke University Press (disability justice)

Being Heumann: An unrepentant memoir of a disability rights activist, Judith Heumann with Kristen Joiner, 2021, Beacon Press (disability rights)

Disability visibility: First-person stories from the twenty-first century, Alice Wong (Ed.), 2020, Knopf Doubleday (disability justice)

Academic ableism: Disability and higher education, Jay Timothy Dolmage, 2017, University of Michigan Press (disability studies)

Ability profiling and school failure: One child's struggle to be seen as competent, Kathleen M. Collins, 2012 (2nd ed.), Routledge (disability studies)

Disability and difference in global contexts: Enabling a transformative body politic, Nirmala Erevelles, 2011, Palgrave Macmillian

What can a body do? How we meet the built world, Sara Hendren, 2020, Riverhead Books

ACADEMIC JOURNAL ARTICLES

Collins, K. & Ferri, B. (2016). Literacy education and disability studies: Reenvisioning struggling students. *Journal of Adolescent & Adult Literacy, 60*(1), 7-12.

Ferri, B. A. & Connor, D. J. (2005). Tools of exclusion: Race, disability, and (re)segregated education. *Teachers College Record, 107*(3), 453-74.

NETFLIX

Special, *Crip Camp*

CHAPTER 5
ARCHITECTURAL UTOPIAS: THE PEDAGOGY OF STILL-EXISTING SOCIALIST INFRASTRUCTURE

Derek R. Ford

DEREK R. FORD is a teacher, organizer, and educational theorist. They've published eight books, the latest of which is *Teaching the Actuality of Revolution* (Iskra, 2023), academic articles in a variety of journals on the fields of art, educational theory, political studies, and music, as well as numerous essays in popular outlets such as *Black Agenda Report, Monthly Review, International Magazine*, and others. They co-edit the Bloomsbury series, *Radical Politics and Education* and are associate editor of *Postdigital Science and Education* and deputy editor of the *Journal for Critical Education Policy Studies*. A member of the editorial collective of the International Manifesto Group and the advisory board of Friends of Socialist China, they serve as the editor for LiberationSchool.org and a contributing editor at the Hampton Institute. They organize with the ANSWER Coalition and the Indianapolis Liberation Center, and other local, national, and international groupings.

DEBATES IN AND AROUND the realm of critical theory on the relationship between art and politics, at least those primarily referenced in academic literature and even social movements of recent decades have, in general, focused primarily on particular forms of "art" such as literature and painting, performance and theater. This is not an absolute proclamation or "a general law," as Gabriel Rockhill puts it, as scholars such as Walter Benjamin, David Harvey, Henri Lefebvre, and those inspired by the latter, including Andy Merrifield, have taken on architectural politics.[1] Moreover, there is no such ontological "thing" as

---

1 Gabriel Rockhill, *Interventions in Contemporary Thought: History, Politics, Aesthetics* (Edinburgh: Edinburgh University Press, 2016), 244.

architecture, for not only do other forms recognized as art entail architectural features—like the organization of a poem or novel—but what comes to be seen as architecture is the result of ongoing struggles of various forces rather than individuals or single social movements. As such, Rockhill's argument is that theoretical engagements on politics and art, particularly in the European and U.S. traditions, "have evidenced a disproportionate interest" in art forms "at the expense of what is commonly recognised as a distinct field of practices, namely those of architecture, building, design, urban planning and public art."[2] Rockhill partly attributes architecture's absence in these conversations to the class standing of those who helped produce the concept of the fine arts and theory, as they were products and producers of "the bourgeois liberal ideals of education" and were accordingly interested in how the works they knew as "fine art" might "contribute to the political struggle that they hoped to instigate or support."[3]

Unlike the "fine arts," however, architecture and the built-environment are overtly engaged in and therefore the ongoing result of direct struggles between a host of forces, from banks and developers to local politicians and hedge funds, neighborhood committees and progressive organizations to the homeless and urban recreationalists. The architecture around us, the pavement, curbs (maybe curb cuts), sidewalks or lack thereof, height and density of buildings, hidden paths, and green spaces, are always dynamic, open to surprises, and either protected or under threat. They are manifestations of struggles for a spatial order and form that creates and recreates, calls attention to, or directly challenges the reproduction and naturalness of the social order. Here ideology is literally concrete, a direct means to enable and constrain our movements and encounters while being *used* in ways that can undermine or usurp the architectural design." As such, architecture could be seen as, in Rockhill's words, "the political art par excellence."[4] Rockhill renders critical theory's lack of engagement with architecture in the art and politics debate visible and provides a quite nuanced and clear historical-materialist analysis for this absent connection. The determinants of the theorists

---

2   Ibid., 246.

3   Ibid., 254, 256.

4   Ibid., 259.

and schools of thought to which Rockhill refers share much in common with those who did and do consider the relationship between art and politics via architecture insofar as they are premised on a rejection of actually-existing socialism.

This article illuminates the significance of aesthetics, architecture, and political struggles by turning to concrete historical examples of socialist urbanism and city planning. In addition to drawing out architecture as a prime exemplar of political art, I find it a useful model for *pedagogical* politics. More specifically, these examples illustrate the inherently political nature of all education and of Paulo Freire's utopian pedagogy. Although some mischaracterize Freire's conception of the educational relationship as one of absolute equality, Freire always maintained the teacher can *start* as a learner but can never stay a learner. To start implies direction, and political pedagogy implies a political direction. The political educator, like the utopian architect, *begins* from learning from the people as part of understanding the current conjuncture. Yet what defines the educator as such is that they *depart from* a certain point toward another [...] there exists within the verb to *start out* a connotation of movement, and another of intentionality, and another of directivity."[5] With this in mind, I turn to the role of architecture and planning in revolutionary pedagogy before turning to concrete examples of political architecture that add an additional element contributing to its status as the exemplary form of political and pedagogical art: its role in the revolutionary process of transforming society and the creation of socialist urbanism, as well as its capacity to endure and persist in the face of counterrevolutions such that, socialist architecture is still with us in "post-socialist" states.

The Politics of Apolitical "Good" Utopian Pedagogy

In education, David Halpin's *Hope and Education* was a noteworthy starting point of utopia's reemergence in educational scholarship, including architectural education. Halpin's utopian realism is half ro-

---

5   Paulo Freire, "South African Freedom Fighter Amilcar Cabral: Pedagogue of the Revolution," trans. S.L. Macrine, F. Naiditch, and J. Paraskeva. In *Critical Pedagogy in Uncertain Times: Hope and Possibility*, ed. S.L. Macrine, (New York: Palgrave Macmillan, 2020), 168-169.

mantic and half pragmatic, resting in the middle ground of piecemeal reforms. Educators, he holds, must insist on the potential for "a specific better future for society" but the *only* social movement through which this is possible is "progressive and patient incremental social reform."[6] Utopian realism is oriented toward "radically progressive conceptions of the future of education" in pursuit of "positive, unusual, but ultimately practicable visions for the form of schools and teaching and learning generally."[7] Halpin's utopic curriculum moves young people from students to "creative learners" defined by their 1) openness to new ideas and experiences; 2) capacity to translate knowledge and skills across different contexts; 3) understanding that learning is or can be hard; and 4) are motivated to redress social problems. Utopian curricula create, Halpin writes, "situations in which pupils are led to create for themselves sustained structures of thinking and meaning around well-chosen subject matter."[8] However, what appears as a combination of movement and direction is, on closer inspection, a subsumption of direction under movement and, hence, a movement *for* movement, a curricular accommodation to the present conjuncture.

Proper utopian education is progressive in the sense that it "takes for granted and promotes a less passive and more active role for the student, who is viewed, with the teacher, as a co-constructor of curriculum and knowledge."[9] The teacher is thus not really a teacher but a fellow learner who demonstrates the endless circle of learning how to remain open to the shifting coordinates of contemporary capitalism. The emphasis on movement and rejection of direction is a product of the intellectual struggle from which Halpin acknowledges his utopian realism emerges. Utopian realism is practical and pragmatic, open and realizable under current conditions unlike "bad" utopianism, which is "ground-

---

6   David Halpin, *Hope and Education: The Role of the Utopian Imagination* (New York: Routledge, 2003), 5.

7   Ibid., 59.

8   Ibid., 114.

9   David Halpin, "Utopian Spaces of 'Robust Hope:' The Architecture and Nature of Progressive Learning Environments," *Asia Pacific Journal of Teacher Education*, 35, no. 3 (2007): 245.

ed in *mere* wistful thinking" to draw "detailed blueprints for change."[10] Bad utopias engage debates about futures that are "impracticable ideal states" whereas good utopias "are capable of transforming it for the better in the future, so as to provide a significant dynamic for action in the here and now."[11] The very invocation, let alone dismissal, of "impracticable states" and therefore of "bad utopias," expresses the maxim there *are* alternatives to the current order, but only ones the current order can accommodate. "Good utopias," then, are not utopias at all.

A similar battle line between bad and good utopianism is drawn in architectural education, where good utopianism is pragmatic, and thus aligned with producing appropriate forms of labor-power for capital, and bad utopianism produces an inability to solve the real problems of the day. For Nathaniel Coleman, architectural education must deal with the troubling omission of utopia from the discipline's curriculum, as architecture entails a *vision* that is often *realized* in built-form. We all grow up in and move through built environments that are pedagogical, teaching and instructing our bodies how we should or must move, how we might move, and the capacities the environment enables and disables in our lives. Utopia and architecture permeate our lives and constitute the web through which our lived experiences and conceptions are produced or degenerated. "Without Utopia," he writes, "architecture and urban design have no vocation other than to adorn capital and its processes."[12] In those cases that the architectural curriculum emphasizes "imaginaries" instead of market-ready skills "the register is primarily *fanciful*, related more to unbuildable projects unburdened by the demands of use," reducing them to theoretical rather than concrete exercises in utopia.[13] Coleman endorses Halpin's conception of utopia as a language of possibility as a progressive step in this direction, seeing architectural education as lacking even the space and time to explore other political and social possibilities.

The main task, Coleman argues, is "to imagine what might be pos-

---

10   Halpin, *Hope and Education*, 39, emphasis added.

11   Ibid.

12   Nathaniel Coleman, "Utopic Pedagogies: Alternatives to Degenerate Architecture," *Utopian Studies*, 23, no. 2 (2012): 315.

13   Ibid., 316.

sible," which depends on understanding what exists, because if what exists is taken as the best there can be, Utopia is meaningless.[14] Coleman rejects "bad utopianism" that totalizes in favor of "good utopianism" that is ephemeral, always under attack, and that serves as examples of possibility rather than blueprints. Despite insisting utopianism is political, then, here Coleman's utopian architectural curriculum is devoid of a political vision, ending up endorsing utopia as a method or over and against utopia as an actuality to be accomplished. Yet in a later article, Coleman argues reclaiming utopian architecture necessitates its position within a social project and political endeavor, on entailing:

> a significant level of detail in the description of what is proposed; elaboration of a positive transformation of social and political life as key to what is proposed or constructed; and, not least, a substantive—ethical and aesthetical—critique of the present informed by a critical-historical perspective.[15]

While his earlier works endorsed the binary utopias, they importantly began by challenging the anti-communist orthodoxy that restrains our present horizons. In sum, then utopia entails both an ephemeral imaginative process but must ultimately be aimed toward and constructed in a built form that is not only *different* but *radically* and, at present, unimaginably better.

Utopian Pedagogy: Open and Closed, Partial and Total

To reclaim the essence of utopia, education must supplement imagination with action, openness with direction or, in Paulo Freire's formulation, the dialectic between *denouncing* and *announcing*. Freire remarked early on that overcoming dehumanization is the utopia of the human in "which they announce in dehumanizing processes."[16] Utopian pedagogy for Freire is a combination of denouncing the present order and announcing a new order, which means it is a process of open-ended

---

14 Ibid., 333.

15 Nathaniel Coleman, "The Problematic of Architecture and Utopia," *Utopian Studies*, 25, no. 1 (2014): 8.

16 Paulo Freire, "Cultural Action and Conscientization," *Harvard Educational Review*, 40, no. 3 (1970): 456.

imagination and wonder but one guided by a political project. This is clear when Freire, in the same early article, qualifies denouncing and announcing in several ways, the most significant of which is a desired ending point. He turns to Marx's distinction between the worst architects and the best bees where Marx separates the worst of the former from the best of the latter because, as good as bees are at constructing their cells and habitats, the worst architect has a vision and a *plan* to build their housing and habitat. Of utopia as the coupling of denouncing and announcing is accompanied by several qualifications, including the need for an endpoint. Freire turns to Marx's definition of the *capitalist* labor process, which *presumes* a distinctively human form of work distinct from other animals. "A spider conducts operations that resemble those of a weaver, and a bee puts to shame many an architect in the construction of her cells," he writes. However, the difference between "the worst architect" and "the best of bees is this, that the architect raises his structure in imagination before he erects it in reality."[17] One who enters a situation intending to teach without a plan—or with a plan to learn with the learners—is, by definition, not a teacher. Utopian education is not an endless dialogue of imaginative potentialities, and the utopian project need not *always* entail or move through dialogical processes; *that* would be wistful thinking.

What should be highlighted is that Freire's praxis isn't presented as and doesn't emerge from pure abstract thinking but concrete situations. Thus, after defining utopian pedagogy Freire applies it to the revolutionary project. The revolutionary utopian pedagogue adopts "their action to historical conditions, taking advantage of the real and unique possibilities that exist" in order "to seek the *most efficient and viable* means of helping the people" accomplish the revolutionary project.[18] The figure that, more than any other, embodies "the pedagogue of the revolution" for Freire is Amílcar Cabral. In the introduction to

---

17   Karl Marx, *Capital: A Critique of Political Economy (Vol. 1): The Process of Capitalist Production*, trans. S. Moore and E. Aveling (New York: International Publishers, 1867/1967), 174. Note that this definition is a presupposition for labor under capitalism and Marx doesn't make a qualitative judgement between humans and other animals overall by, for example, merely stating humans are better than bees.

18   Freire, "Cultural Action and Conscientization," 470, emphasis added.

Pedagogy in Process—a series of letters to the Republic's Commissioner of State for Education and Culture, Mario Cabral, and bookended by his reflections on his visits there—Freire acknowledges Cabral as a prophet because he started with the real concrete or "what was actually true" and not with the ideal concrete or "what he might wish were true" whenever "he both denounced and announced. Denunciation and annunciation in Amílcar Cabral were never disassociated from each other, just as they were never outside the revolutionary process."[19] Freire's first public talk after his exile from Brazil makes it even clearer how Cabral helped Freire's formulation of utopian pedagogy.

He recalls a discussion with an educational worker who fought with and under Amílcar Cabral in the anti-Portuguese national liberation struggle. Freire asked what was most impressive to him in his experiences with Cabral. The young man answers: his imagination, or "his capacity to know beyond his immediate surroundings and to imagine the not yet." Freire didn't understand, and eventually, the comrade provided Freire with a concrete example, one of Cabral's seminars delivered at military encampments during the armed struggle. At this lecture, delivered after an intensive air-bombing campaign Cabral gathered the fighters together for a lecture (not a dialogue). Knowing the bombs could start dropping again at any moment, Cabral directed to shift 200 troops out of the frontlines "to send to a different battlefront. I need two hundred of you to send to Guinea-Conakry, to the Capacitation Institute" so they could return "to the liberated zones, in order to work as teachers."[20] The political and military struggle was against the present order but for a new one, and thus Cabral recognized the necessity of dialectical utopianism but within a concrete praxis. The built-spaces and the aesthetic configuration during the struggle and after its accomplishment were, as always, deeply pedagogical.

Architectural utopian pedagogy for Freire is enabled by, reflective of, and generative toward actually-existing projects, imperfect as they may be and unattainable as all utopias must be to qualify as such. For

---

19   Paulo Freire, *Pedagogy in Process: Letters to Guinea-Bissau* (London: Bloomsbury, 1978), 11.

20   Freire, "South African Freedom Fighter Amilcar Cabral: Pedagogue of the Revolution," 164.

this reason, it is worthwhile pointing out that the dominant narrative of Paulo Freire's praxis as the starting point of critical pedagogy is historically inaccurate and theoretically unsound, which means we should be cautious of importing critical theory as it presents itself into other projects.[21] Architectural utopian pedagogy must entail an educational mode in which possibilities are opened and horizons expanded but within an overall political objective to be accomplished. Yet Freire demonstrates these are not only the "not-yet" but the "already" or "actually-existing" materials of our present, which necessarily includes our past. We can now turn to examine these present alternatives that persist in our present thanks to the work of recent scholars working to overcome the anti-communist dogma of the academy.

Still-Socialist Architecture Outlasts Actually-Existing Capitalism

While the "base-superstructure" model plays a far outsized role in Marxism, Michal Murawski taught me its significance as a pedagogical and aesthetic metaphor.[22] "The German words translated into base and superstructure," he writes, carry "explicitly architectural connotations." Even as architectural praxis must engage with land and spatial property, it does so in a way that delinks property from infrastructure, which is odd because that infrastructure of urbanism "constitutes the key site of the making and unmaking of socialism" because socialist social relations and their spatial form are predicated on the expropriation of the property of the expropriators.[23] The production of socialist cities and the built environment are physical manifestations of Marxism and a socialist society "planned and drawn on paper; rendered in stone, wood, glass, ce-

---

21   See, for example, as, for example, the recent and solid paper, Cameron McEwan, "Architectural Pedagogy for the Anthropocene: Theory, Critique and Typological Urbanism," *Archnet-IJAR*, **ahead of print**.

22   See Derek Ford, "The Base-Superstructure: A Model for Analysis and Action," *Liberation School*, 22 November 2021, available here: https://www.liberationschool.org/base-superstructure-introduction.

23   Michal Murawski. (2018). "Marxist Morphologies: A Materialist Critique of Brute Materialities, Flat Infrastructures, Fuzzy Property an Complexified Cities." *Focaal*, 82, no. 1 (2018): 17, 19.

ment, and concrete; and filled with life, with living entities who were, by inhabiting and using these cities and buildings, engaged in the process of becoming socialist themselves."[24] Given that socialist revolutions occurred not where capitalism was most developed—as Marx's critique of capital seemed to indicate—but where it was least developed, once the expropriators were expropriated the new governments had to not merely collectivize ownership of the means of production and reproduction, but produce them as well.

Because socialist revolutions have, thus far, occurred not where capitalism and its contradictions were the most developed but where the capitalist class was weakest, revolutionary states had and have to address a deluge of overwhelming problems from underdevelopment and colonialism to the absence of basic infrastructure and literacy. In the first socialist state, what soon became the Soviet Union, cities were key spaces and mechanisms to take on such tasks simultaneously. Through a particular kind of urban planning, they could not only develop productive forces but also create a new set of social relations, a new collectivity and socialist spirit. It should go without saying that socialist urbanism manifested in various iterations and phases across concrete situations. Many could appear or even take a similar form as the capitalist urbanization that accompanied capitalist industrialization. Take the "company town" model, a space organized around a specific corporation or industry, which developed in opposing socialist systems. The *content*, however, manifested their antagonisms, for in the U.S. they were unplanned, unregulated, and designed purely for the pursuit of profit, in the Soviet Union they were *socialist* towns insofar as they were planned with the needs of the people (in the town and beyond) in mind and didn't generate profits for a small group of owners, among other differences.

Mark Smith argues the transition away from this model was due largely to the obstacle posed by scale, in size and in distance, as implementing this model in rural areas was technically difficult and created social antagonisms. There is no doubt that isolated districts would tend to encourage individual rather than collective identities. Another likely factor had to do with the evolution of the Soviet system and economy, particularly after their defeat of the Nazis in World War II. Implement-

---

24   Ibid., 20.

ing pre-planned towns in this way, however, could not but hamper the collectivity central to socialist ideology. Moreover, as the Soviet Union rebuilt itself and its new and old allies, their forces of production developed quite rapidly, enabling an increasing specialization and division of labor within and between different cities and states. From the ashes of the socialist town came the microdistrict, or *microrayon*, the form of socialist urbanism that endured and spread throughout the world during the mid-late 20th century and still exists in some states and sites today.

Among the various forces contributing to this model and its ability to spread and expand in dynamic ways was, of course, the collective spirit of the people but, more pertinent to this article, the utopianism integral to Soviet architectural imagination. As Kimberly Elman Zarecor argues, blueprints for microdistricts were drawn up "years before there were material, financial, or labor resources to support their construction" such that socialism is "always a future-looking and aspirational ideology."[25] What seemed utopian one decade was realized—or realizable in the next—thereby extending the socialist horizon's actuality and distance. Freire's utopianism is also a kind of dialectic of excavation (digging into the present and past) and architecture (projecting or announcing a future). Such dynamism is emphasized in Murawki's study, addressed shortly, which focuses on Poland. As the Nazi forces decimated Poland and its capital city, communist architects were already envisioning designs for a future city the architects themselves wrote, in 1935, appeared "purely utopian" insofar as it required collective control over the land the planning—and therefore the expropriation of the expropriators—but within 10 years the "purely utopian" foundations "move quickly from 'theoretical premises' to implementation."[26] The infrastructure, itself determined by the global class war at the time, determined the concrete dreams and plans of utopian socialism.

As the relations within and between the socialist camp developed such that each socialist city could occupy a thread in a fabric of pro-

---

25   Kimberly Elman Zarecor, "What was so Socialist about the Socialist City? Second World Urbanity in Europe," *Journal of Urban History*, 44, no. 1 (2018): 101.

26   Michal Murawski, *The Palace Complex: A Stalinist Skyscraper, Capitalist Warsaw, and a City Transformed* (Bloomington: Indiana University Press, 2019), 44.

duction with their own specializations as part of a coordination within and between states. This company town, in a sense, overcame its barriers and "expanded outward geographically and through increased industrial production multiplied their economic effects" such that "any one of these cities then also had the possibility to become a site of expansion."[27] No longer a single factory or even industry, microdistricts were neighborhood-scale cities occupied by between 5,000 and, at the limit, 20,000 inhabitants planned not only to maximize walking space but to provide the educational and recreational services, collective kitchens, nurseries, factories parks, and so on desired and appropriated by its inhabitants.

The microdistrict, which was adopted in 1958 as the general framework for socialist urbanism by the Congress of International Union Architects, differed in both form and content from capitalist modernization. When utopianism entered architecture and city planning in 19th century Europe, it attacked the winding roads and narrow streets with diverse towns with wide boulevards to smooth and hasten the circulation of commodities and accelerate capital's expansion. In the early 20th century, the resulting concentration of urban populations led to the fear of the proletarian masses and their chaos. Capitalist architecture—represented best by Le Corbusier—knew it couldn't eliminate the laborers (because it needed their commodity of labor-power) and worked to restrain or contain it through functionalist planning and limiting encounters or public spaces. To be sure, this wasn't uniform, as social-democratic states provided mass housing and basic rights of the residents to inhabit their own cities (unlike, say, the capitalist states like the U.S). Socialist urbanism, on the other hand, was based on *micro*districts, each representing a node in an expansive and expandable centrality. Housing wasn't an afterthought but a guiding principle or "a material infrastructure," so that "new factories were not built without proposals for additional housing and neighborhood services."[28] Microdistricts worked to facilitate socialist relations by *providing* spaces for encounters with differences.

---

27   Zarecor, "What was so Socialist about the Socialist City?" 102.

28   Kimberly Elman Zarecor, "What was so Socialist about the Socialist City? Second World Urbanity in Europe," *Journal of Urban History*, 44, no. 1 (2018): 106.

Intentionally designed to overcome the capitalist ideology of the private individual and the subjugation of women to reproductive labor in the household, they were the opposite of suburban sprawl and chaotic urbanism under U.S. racist capitalism in which the city (re)produces white supremacy and class inequality, Soviet microdistricts *embodied* a collective sense of equality in built-form. Smith notes that "all kinds of people lived in the microdistricts. The doctor and accountant brushed up against the factory worker and the cleaner."[29] Even if they *looked* like repetitive prefabricated high-rises, what happened in the microdistricts was anything but monotonous, homogenous, or segregated. Here the content and form of urbanism clearly worked toward overcoming the division of mental and manual labor, as evidenced by the social backgrounds of the membership of the leading bodies of the Communist Party of the Soviet Union: the Politburo and Central Committee. Whereas in the U.S. only the children of the elite have a chance at political positions of power, in the USSR the vast majority of its leaders emerged from social groups outside of "Party elites." As Albert Szymanski notes, one 1966 study of the 74 percent of Central Committee members with available information, "36 per cent had manual working-class parents, 47 per cent peasant parents and only 16 per cent non-manual (i.e. either intelligentsia or low-level white collar) parents."[30]

The expansion of microdistricts in the Soviet Union also worked to overcome the division between the town and country. As Smith notes, the first "Stalinist" town organized around a production or firm wasn't so distinct from the countryside. This is not only because of the infrastructure that connected them but because of internal migration and the blending of factory and agriculture, such that "many factories effectively ran their own farms, without which they would have been unable to feed their workers."[31] In the end, Smith disproves the "socialism failed" narrative by arguing that, while reductive, the primary distinction between socialist urbanism (in the USSR) and capitalist urbanism was the

---

29 Mark B. Smith, "Faded Red Paradise: Welfare and the Soviet City after 1953," *Contemporary European History*, 24, no. 4 (2015): 605.

30 Albert Szymanski, *Is the Red Flag Flying? The Political Economy of the Soviet Union Today* (London: Zed Books, 1979), 74.

31 Smith, "Faded Red Paradise," 614.

presence of equality and the relations of property.

Zarecor's research leads to the same conclusion. What, if anything, differentiated the similar appearance of prebuilt mass housing in capitalist or socialist Germany, for example? It is easy to point out the differences between housing in the Soviet Union and the segregated U.S., but what about social-democratic European countries? Zarecor insists it wasn't the degree of specialization or the quality of the materials or products. Her conclusion coincides with other case studies demonstrating "that it was more than just the formal expression and urban design of the cities that made them socialist but also the social relations and sense of community that they consciously produced."[32] Put plainly, the primary difference was that socialist cities were part of an architectural totality and socialist urbanism was premised on the revolution of social relations within that totality in a revolutionary direction of equality and egalitarianism. This was a through-line not limited only to the era of the microdistrict. As Smith—no fan of the Soviet Union—argues, "one could even claim that the concept which was most Soviet about the company town was equality."[33] Based on interviews, he argues this sense of equality and collectivity existed until the overthrow of the Soviet Union; existed even in the last days of the first manifestation of socialism.

Conclusion: The Pedagogy of Still-Socialist Architecture

However, socialism etched in built-form, socialism and infrastructure, is not so easily wiped out, which is what makes Murawski's research so fascinating. His object of inquiry is Poland's Palace of Culture and Science and the surrounding Parade Park in contemporary Warsaw. The towering skyscraper is 42-stories tall and until 2022 was the largest structure in Poland. The goal wasn't (only) monumental height but the production of a space through which social difference could encounter each other as even in 2015 it included numerous theaters for performances and screenings, universities, a Congressional Hall with several thousand seems, the War City Assembly room, a Palace of Youth, in addition to dance schools and entertainment facilities. The sheer verticality of the

---

32   Zarecor, "What was so Socialist about the Socialist City?" 109.
33   Smith, "Faded Red Paradise," 604.

Palace *was* important insofar as socialist realism rejected modernist abstraction in favor of "a much more *hierarchical, symmetrical,* and *holistic* relationship between the absolute center of the city and its remaining parts."[34] Whereas capitalist skyscrapers are built on speculation, for profit, and without any planning or care as to its effect on the totality of the environment or social relations in which it is built, socialist tall buildings were constructed where they were needed and "fulfilled public or residential functions rather than revenue-accumulating ones" with a form guided not by exchange-value but by use-value, and constructed in order to synthesize the dialectic of the everyday and the totality.

The Warsaw Palace was not only modeled on the planned but never constructed Supreme Palace of the Soviets, but on similar architectural forms that united heterogeneous elements in a building or complex and were, like collective residential neighborhoods called microdistricts produced across the socialist camp. Guided by the need to produce a *collectivity* out of a fragmented and isolated set of individuals or families and other restrictive social groupings, microdistricts housed diverse groupings of workers and families who regularly encountered each other through shared educational, leisure, green, residential, food, commercial, and cultural spaces. The Palace functioned similarly, as a physical space for formal and informal encounters partly through the condensation of various cultural and social sites, partly through its vast size and the surrounding park, but most importantly because it was founded on the expropriation of expropriated property.

Since the capitalist counterrevolution, the Palace and its surroundings have been subjected to intense debate. It still stands, Murawski holds, because it not only *represents* a vision of an alternative society but is a concrete manifestation of one. "The palace," as he puts it, isn't a relic of socialism in a capitalist city but a "still-socialist one" that, because of "the economic aesthetic and public spirit built into it by its designers— is able to endure as an enclave off a noncapitalist aesthetic, spatial, and social world at the heart of a late capitalist city." He even suggests it can still function as a "socialist horizon" for the country.[35] This isn't a return to a past but the concrete present out of which not only alternatives, not

---

34   Murawski, *The Palace Complex*, 46.
35   Ibid., 271.

only possibilities of alternatives, but *real, existing, and more just alternatives* are dreamt and materialized. Utopia is not only a process, not only an aspiration, but an *actuality*, and together these constitute the real "stuff" of curricular utopias in our conjuncture.

SECTION 3
Theories, Strategies, & Tactics

CHAPTER 6
HISTORICAL MATERIALISM: A POSTDIGITAL PHILOSOPHICAL METHOD

Summer Pappachen

SUMMER PAPPACHEN is a Ph.D. student in political theory and political economy at Northwestern University, where she also works as a teacher's assistant. She is a Bargaining Committee Member for Local 1122, Northwestern University Graduate Workers—United Electric (NUGW-UE). Amidst bargaining for 3000 graduate workers' historic first contract, she also organizes with the Chicago Liberation Center, helping connect the struggles and dreams of the working people in her city with those of our siblings around the world. Her scholarship has been published in academic outlets and popular outlets such as *Monthly Review*, *Liberation School*, and *Breaking the Chains*.

Introduction

WHAT IS THE *POSTDIGITAL*? To us, it is both an era and a phase. If the digital marked the large-scale transformations brought on by the universalization of computerization, the *post*digital names the afterlife of that universalization. We currently live in a postdigital era marked by the aftereffects of the universalization of computerization into nearly every aspect of material life. We also live in the postdigital phase where the logics of the digital operate on a metaphorical level. Gabriel Rockhill explains that while eras mark "a historical time period," phases are "always distributed in a precise manner across time as well as in space and in society."[1] So while eras are historical periods, phases are metaphorical logics with no temporal loyalty.[2] Petar Jandrić reminds us that "forms of

---

1 Gabriell Rockhill, *Counter-History of the Present: Untimely Interrogations into Globalization, Technology, Democracy* (Durham. NC: Duke University Press, 2017), 4.

2 For instance, when someone says, "She's in her blue hair phase" we know

binary code are found in ancient texts in China and India," and that in an era long before written language, binary code was found "in various forms of communication such as smoke signals and drums."[3] In this paper, I am interested in the postdigital as a *phase*—as a logic which comes and goes from the limelight. Put another way, I am interested in postdigital research rather than just research in the postdigital era.

In particular, I am interested in searching for philosophical methods of postdigital research. Our search has led us to an old friend found anew: to historical materialism. Early postdigital theorist Geoff Cox reminds us that time, too, is ideological, and one way it is conceptualized is in a historicist way: by viewing the past as a "continuum of progress" teleologically leading to an end, that end being the present. Cox ultimately "tasks" historical materialism with "revealing the inner workings of historicism as an ideological construction."[4] I take inspiration from this provocation, and argue for a return to Marx and the communist tradition to demonstrate that historical materialism *is* a postdigital research method. It is with a sense of urgency that I offer historical materialism as a postdigital method of philosophy. In a time of deepening suffering for most working people of the world, I argue that postdigital researchers must combine theoretical forces with Marxists, unite disparate apparatuses, and build a united research front that can take on the postdigital challenges that lie ahead of us.

In this article, the first section defines historical materialism through its most popular iteration: the base-superstructure model. I show that in contrast to misleading interpretations, base-superstructure was always intended to serve as a tool for presentation and teaching rather than explanation. In the second section, through a text-based close reading of base-superstructure, I show that instead of being historicist (often

---

that this phase can end and come back again—tied not to chronological time but to a certain characteristic. In America in 2023, young people often comedically call phases eras, like by saying "I'm in my blue hair era," hinting at the comedy of calling a passing phase a distinct historic period.

3   Petar Jandrić, "The Three Ages of the Digital," in *Keywords in Radical Philosophy and Education* ed. Derek Ford (Leiden: Brill/Sense, 2019), 162.

4   Geoff Cox, "Postscript on the Post-Digital and the Problem of Temporality," in *Postdigital Aesthetics: Art, Computation and Design* ed. David M. Berry and Michael Dieter (London: Palgrave Macmillan, 2015), 155.

charged with economic determinism, stageism, and linear developmentalism), historical materialism has always been anti-historicist and temporally open. In the third and final section, I look at the rise of bioinformational capitalism, and at historical materialism's curiously biological lens. Given that the challenges we face today are deeply biological, and given historical materialism's serendipitous twin birth with evolutionary biology in the 1800s, the marxist method presents as an especially fit postdigital philosophical method.

Base-Superstructure as a Teaching Metaphor

Students are often taught Marxist methodology through the base-superstructure model. In our classrooms, a close reading of historical materialism is substituted for an easy explanation of the base-superstructure model. It often goes something like this: there is an underground "material base" with an aboveground "superstructure," with the base causally producing the superstructure and, in more generous interpretations, the superstructure reacting back upon the base. In this section, I will show this to be a misconception, even if it is not an unforgivable or nonsensical one. It is not nonsensical given the overall lack of engagement with Marx's work and marxist theory overall, which would reveal the strange, outsized role the base-superstructure model plays in discussions about historical materialism.

We can begin to rectify this misconception by turning to Marx's famous articulation of the relationship between the base and superstructure. In *A Contribution to the Critique of Political Economy*, Marx summarizes the "general conclusion" of his study, which will be worth revisiting in its entirety:

In the social production which men carry on they enter into definite relations that are indispensable and independent of their will; these relations of production correspond to a definite stage of development of their material powers of production. The sum total of these relations of production constitutes the economic structure of society—the real foundation, on which rise legal and political superstructures and to which correspond definite forms of social consciousness. The mode of production of material life determines the general character of the social, political and spiritual processes of life. It is not the consciousness of men that determines their existence, but, on the contrary, their social existence determines their consciousness.[5]

Here the economic structure is defined in contrast to the legal and political superstructures. A very specific reading of these passages contributes heavily to the dominant understanding of the base and superstructure today—deployed by both marxists and our opponents—as a mechanical dogma or, at best, as an explanatory mechanism. In opposition, I argue that base and superstructure is a metaphor: a way to analyze and approach society and social transformation rather than a simple explanation. Rather than being an *explanation*, I argue that it is a way to *present* Marx and Engels' findings about how to approach the study of society. The book from which the above passages are drawn, *A Contribution to the Critique of Political Economy*, was a short and popularly-written book meant to be more educational than theoretical. Given that this was one of only two explicit mentions of the base-superstructure in Marx's entire oeuvre,[6] it indicates something about his intentions in using it.

Engels explains this in a 1890 letter to a German socialist Joseph Bloch who wrote to him, asking if he and Marx meant for it to seem like "the production and reproduction of actual life [are] alone the determining factors" in historical materialism?[7] Engels replied that, "According to the materialist conception of history, the ultimately determining element in history is the production and reproduction of real life," emphasizing a temporal element—it is not the only, but it is the "last."[8] He goes on, "If somebody twists this into saying that the economic factor

---

5   Karl Marx, *A Contribution to the Critique of Political Economy*, trans. N.I. Stone (Chicago, IL: Charles H. Kerr & Company, 1859/1904), 11-12.

6   The other place is in *The Eighteenth Brumaire of Louis Bonaparte*: "Upon the different forms of property, upon the social conditions of existence, rises an entire superstructure of distinct and peculiarly formed sentiments, illusions, modes of thought, and views of life. The entire class creates and forms them out of its material foundations and out of the corresponding relations."

7   Frederick Engels, "Engels to Joseph Bloch" (Peking: Foreign Languages Press, 1878), 74.

8   Ibid., 75.

is the only determining one, he is transforming that proposition into a meaningless, abstract, absurd phrase."⁹ He even takes responsibility for the fact that, "the younger people sometimes lay more stress on the economic side than is due to it" insofar as "we had to emphasize the main principle over and against our adversaries, who denied it."¹⁰ I interpret this as a reminder that Marx and Engels were not only theorists but also teachers, making pedagogical decisions about how best to present their ideas to working people. They placed special emphasis on the economic base because they were teaching against those who denied the determination of productive relations altogether. The 1800s were a time of great idealism in philosophy which assumed that ideas determine the nature of our existence, as opposed to materialism which reminds us that the nature of our existence determines our ideas. Thus, Marx and Engels' emphasis on the economic should not be seen as an abstract and absolute statement but as a particular and timed one. Their intervention embodies the ethic of historical materialism by being attuned to the needs of their historical conjuncture (the particular combination of forces and events in play in a specific time and place). Rather than giving a timeless, abstract explanation, the model was intended as a timed and conjunctural teaching metaphor.

For an example of the conjuncture in which they were entering, we can look to the second place in Marx's oeuvre where he explicitly mentions the superstructure. In *The Eighteenth Brumaire of Louis Bonaparte*, Marx applies the metaphor to a practical analysis of the French social-democratic party which was a central political voice in the mid-1800s.[11] The base-superstructure metaphor helped him describe the social democrats' role in the failure of the 1848 Paris revolution and the success of the 1851 coup of Louis Napoleon Bonaparte. He deployed it to "distinguish still more the phrases and fancies of parties from their real organism and their real interests, their conception of themselves from their reality."[12] Despite their revolutionary phrases, social democracy, he

---

9   Ibid., 75.

10   Ibid., 78.

11   Kark Marx, *The Eighteenth Brumaire of Louis Bonaparte* (New York: International Publishers, 1852/1972).

12   Ibid., 47.

writes, "is epitomized in the fact that democratic-republican institutions are demanded as a means, not of doing away with two extremes, capital and wage labor, but of weakening the antagonism and transforming it into harmony."[13] The social-democratic forces didn't seek to overthrow the existing relations of production but to manage them in a more equitable manner through the capitalist superstructure. They didn't seek to overthrow the base, just the superstructure. They operated solely in the superstructure—hoping for "sentiments, illusions, modes of thought, and views of life" to bring about improvement in society while keeping the "social conditions of existence" of the masses unchanged.[14]

Base-Superstructure as an Anti-Historicist, Temporal Metaphor

Geoff Cox tasked historical materialism with "revealing the inner workings of historicism as an ideological construction."[15] Yet historical materialism (articulated through the base-superstructure model) has often been accused of that which it has been tasked to challenge. We need not look hard through literature published in various humanities and social science disciplines to find charges of historicism, economism, determinism, and linear developmentalism. In critical educational research, for instance, these charges are repeated *ad nauseam* (often without specific quotations or even references to Marx). For one classic example, Henry Giroux announces his theory of educational resistance by contrasting it with "reproduction accounts of schooling" that "have continually patterned themselves after structural-functionalist versions of Marxism which stress that history is made "behind the backs of the members of society," thereby diminishing or eliminating "the importance of human agency and the notion of resistance."[16] Here we see the marxist method characterized as deleting human agency and contingency from history.

---

13 Ibid., 50.

14 Ibid., 47.

15 Cox, "Postscript on the Post-Digital and the Problem of Temporality," 155.

16 Henry Giroux, "Theories of Reproduction and Resistance in the New Sociology of Education: A Critical Analysis," *Harvard Educational Review* 53, no. 3 (1983): 259.

For another example from critical educational research, Clayton Pierce legitimates his work on W. E. B. Du Bois and education by affirming that "the U.S. education system cannot simply be explained through its relation to economic superstructure or how schools operate solely to reproduce economic social relations beneficial to the processes of capitalist accumulation."[17] Here we see historical materialism being characterized as tunnel visioned on economic forces and profit accumulation. In both cases, Marx and historical materialism are delivered to us as simple economic determinism, a delivery accomplished by superficial or cursory glosses at the primary source material.

A close reading of the primary source material reveals something else altogether. In the preface to *A Contribution to the Critique of Political Economy*, a few lines after the passage quoted at length in the last section, Marx writes that revolutionary transformations occur because of a conflict within the base—a conflict between "the material forces of production" and "the existing relations of production, or—what is but a legal expression for the same thing—with the property relations within which they had been at work before."[18] Once transformation begins "with the change of the economic foundation," then "the entire immense superstructure is more or less rapidly transformed."[19] Here we see that the base of society—also translated as "infrastructure"—includes the productive forces and the relations of production. Productive forces can be the factory, the labor-power, the machines used by the workers, the raw materials they work with. The relations of production can be the social organization of production and reproduction, or how the re/production of life is structured, including laws about property rights. As such, the base doesn't just consist of the forces of production, but productive relations. These relations are not only economic but also necessarily social.

Furthermore, the superstructure comprises the political-legal system of the state and consciousness—or ideology, yet the superstructure

---

17 Clayton Pierce, "W.E.B. Du Bois and Caste Education: Racial Capitalist Schooling from Reconstruction to Jim Crow," *American Educational Research Journal* 54, no. 1S (2017): 28.

18 Karl Marx, *A Contribution to the Critique of Political Economy*, 12.

19 Ibid., 12.

is also economic insofar as the state and ideology are themselves economic processes. For example, the relations of production require the legal court system and a police force to enforce private property rights. In this instance, the superstructure is crucial to the reproduction of the base. Because the capitalist court system arises from capitalist relations of production, changes in the court system or police force might alter the existing relations of production, even if they can't fundamentally overthrow them, for that requires the creation of a new social and economic system. In practice, for Marx, this meant he opposed the absorption of the people's project into capitalist circuits of management, but it did not mean opposing life-saving reforms within capitalism.[20] Instead he believed that changes to the superstructure and base—already intertwined—must be pursued in tandem, with the ultimate objective of overthrowing the capitalist system. In other words, reform and revolution must be pursued in tandem.

Instead of viewing historical materialism as a historicist or economistic, we are better served to recognize it as a temporal metaphor. In his letter to Bloch, Engels writes that the economy determines "in the last instance."[21] He repeats this phrasing in a correspondence with German economist Conrad Schmidt: he writes, only "in the last instance [is] production the decisive factor."[22] Here the spatial metaphor (above/below, or inside/outside) is transformed into a temporal one. Not only is the image of a building and its steel infrastructure invoked, but so is the notion of a sequence of events.[23]

Althusser picks up on this idea and develops it further by restating

---

20   In *Capital*, Marx ended his famous chapter 'On the Working Day' (detailing the horrific consequences of British industrialization for workers, peasants, and slaves) by calling for the oppressed to organize and institute legal reforms which limited the length of the working day. Out of the seeds of this struggle, in which Marx participated, British workers eventually won the eight-hour day which predominates globally to this day.

21   Engels, "Engels to Joseph Bloch," 75.

22   Engels, "Engels to Joseph Conrad" (Peking: Foreign Languages Press, 1878), 80.

23   Derek Ford and Maria Esposito, "Aesthetic Encounters Beyond the Present: Historical Materialism and Sonic Pedagogies for Resisting Abstraction," *Journal for Critical Education Policy Studies* 19, no. 3 (2021): 32–55.

the model as a two-part formulation. He has argued that the base-superstructure model has two contradictory components: while it is true that "the economy is determinant in the last instance" it is also true that "the lonely hour of the 'last instance' never comes."[24] The lonely hour of the "last instance" never comes because there is never a time and space where the pure-economy even exists. The economy never operates alone. As I have shown, it is always fusing and separating from the social: from race, gender, ideas, consciousness, the law, the courts, the police, etc. More fundamentally, the economic is only a product of our thought. Just like the digital is a line we have drawn around certain things in an analog world, the economy too is a line we have drawn about certain parts of reality. One can't actually "see" where the economy ends and where society begins because one can't see the economy or society. The base-superstructure helps us see these invisible lines and relations, as all metaphors do.

There is a persistent absence of the determinant primacy of the material basis within historical materialism. The marxist claim that the material basis takes a primary determining role can be read as a dogma or formula, as a claim about the ubiquity of capitalist social formations across time and space.[25] Or it could be read in the exact opposite fashion, as a claim about the impossibility of such a determination, which exposes politics and philosophy to a radical and foundational contingency operating on the basis of a true historical materialism that "is ready at any moment to stop time."[26]

The concept of the postdigital has always resisted any precise temporal placement, and historical materialism accommodates for that. Like the postdigital, historical materialism disavows linear, purely chronological time, as that is in large part what dialectics means in a historical context. Writing about postdigital aesthetics, Cox reminds us that "[i]t is the temporal sense of incompleteness that drives transformative agency" because "human subjects seek to modify their lived circumstances

---

24 Louis Althusser, *For Marx*, trans. B Brewster (New York: Verso, 1965), 113.

25 Georgio Agamben, *Infancy and history: On the destruction of experience*, trans. L. Leron (New York: Verso, 1987/2007), 105.

26 Ibid., 115.

knowing their experiences to be incomplete."²⁷ In other words, time's incompleteness is where human agency exists. For instance, the relationship between capitalism and socialism is not "a short circuit between otherwise historically clearly separated times" but one of "feedback loops" that allow historical subjects to choose what elements from the old system they want to take with them, and what they want to abolish and create anew.²⁸

The Biology of Historical Materialism

Thus far I have suggested that, like the postdigital, historical materialism can embody a radical temporal openness. I have hinted that historical materialism and postdigitalism are compatible in the temporal realm. In this next section, I turn to consider how historical materialism is specifically biodigital in form. Freeman Dyson has claimed that the twentieth century was the century of physics and the twenty-first century is the century of biology.²⁹ He declared us to be in a biodigital era of capitalism. Michael Peters builds on this observation by carving out the concept of "bioinformational capitalism"—that our current era is defined by capitalist innovations "that control, change and experiment with the material basis of life."³⁰ Bioinformational capitalism is marked by the increasingly central place artificial intelligence, machine learning, data harvesting, bioengineering, biotechnology etc. in the social system. Whether it be through facial recognition data, fingerprint data, genetic data, data our feelings and desire, capitalism has become "obsessed" with "working people's biologies" as a resource for generating surplus value.³¹

Given that the challenges we face in the postdigital era are deeply bi-

---

27   Cox, "Postscript on the Post-Digital and the Problem of Temporality," 160.

28   Ibid.

29   Freeman Dyson, "Our biotech future," *The New York Review* (2007).

30   Michael Peters, "Bio-informational capitalism," *Thesis Eleven* 110, no.1) (2012): 98.

31   Summer Pappachen and Derek Ford, "Spreading Stupidity: Intellectual Disability and Anti-imperialist Resistance to Bioinformational Capitalism," in *Bioinformational Philosophy and Postdigital Knowledge Ecologies* ed. Michael Peters, Petar Jandrić, Sarah Hayes (2022): 242.

ological, historical materialism is a surprisingly fitting method. For one, the base-superstructure model helps us track the bio-oriented changes in the capitalist system. It helps us see that while radical transformations are taking place, they aren't changes *between* modes of production but changes *within* the mode of production. The new theories that have emerged to capture contemporary capital—from bioinformational capitalism to data capitalism, to algorithmic capitalism, to communicative capitalism—aren't tracking changes that have overthrown the base, but changes which are modifying and strengthening it. And second, the flexibility of the base-superstructure model provides an important avenue for describing the role of bioinformation, data, and algorithms in reproducing our exploitation and oppression which is both economic and social. Under bioinformational capitalism, it becomes difficult to distinguish between everyday biological life and the new relations of production which have attached to it. The base and superstructure commingle through the bioinformational set-up of capital. Historical materialism can capture the union of biology, society, and knowledge represented by the postdigital in the same way it captures change between emerging forms of capitalism since the 1800s.

On a methodological level as well, historical materialism is particularly well suited to study biology in an age where it has become a central means for capitalist exploitation. Historical materialism and evolutionary biology were like sisters separated at birth, or at least their mothers thought so. When Marx published *Capital*, he intended to dedicate his book to Charles Darwin who published the *Origin of Species* only eight years prior. They were contemporaries, and Marx saw a deep similarity between their approaches to the empirical world. There was an exchange of amicable letters between the two giants in 1873 where Marx offered to dedicate *Capital* to Darwin.[32] In an important footnote in *Capital*, Marx likens his analysis of the changes in manufacturing tools to how Darwin explained the evolution of organs in plants and animals.[33] He refers to Darwin's work as "epochmaking" for how it used material evi-

---

32 Margaret Fay, "Did Marx Offer to Dedicate Capital to Darwin? A Reassessment of the Evidence," *Journal of the History of Ideas* 39, no. 1 (1978): 135.

33 Karl Marx, *Capital: A Critique of Political Economy, Vol. 1* (New York: International Publishers, 1867), 323.

dence to explain the historical development of species.[34] He saw himself as doing the same thing, but with the social world.

Engels also adopted a biological methodology, perhaps more explicitly than Marx. Engels went so far with the science analogies that sometimes it can read like scientism, like when he compares class antagonism to the repulsion of oxygen and hydrogen molecules.[35] Another point of connection is the title of Engels' *Origin of the Family, Private Property and the State*, which certainly owes something to Darwin's *Origin of Species*. Engels makes all of this explicit during his funeral oration at Marx's graveside in 1883. He said, "Just as Darwin discovered the law of evolution in organic nature, so Marx discovered the law of evolution in human history."[36]

Immersed as we are in an era of bioinformation, historical materialism likely experiences a return to its own beginnings. Bioinformational capitalism—"based on a self-organizing and self-replicating code that harnesses both the results of the information and new biology revolutions"—is comfortable new ground for this old method.[37] Interestingly, this biological sensibility can help us better understand historical materialism in two ways.

For one, Marxist methods are accused of presenting changes in history as the result of organic, inexorable laws. Political scientist Karl Popper for instance points to the few moments where Marx uses the phrase "inexorable laws of Nature" to make this charge.[38] He claimed that Marxism was basically "scientific fortune telling" and "large-scale historical prophecy" because it held that natural laws governed human life.[39] An example could be that capitalism inevitably runs in devastating

---

34 Ibid.

35 Frederick Engels, "Socialism: Utopian and Scientific.," in *The Marx-Engels Reader*, ed. Robert Tucker (New York: W.W. Norton, n.d.), 708.

36 Margaret Fay, "Did Marx Offer to Dedicate *Capital* to Darwin?" (1978): 133.

37 Peters, "Bio-informational capitalism," (2012), 105.

38 Marx, *Capital* (1867), 715.

39 Karl Popper, *The Open Society and Its Enemies* (Princeton, Oxford: Princeton University Press), 279.

boom and bust cycles about which humans can do little. While Marxists *do* see this as a law, biology itself teaches us that laws are not inviolable or standardized. No laws or tendencies, whether in the natural sciences or in the courts, are permanent or fixed. All laws change over time, change depending on environmental conditions, are interpreted differently, applied differently, modified and augmented in innumerable ways.[40] The law of gravity, for instance, while true, is not fixed and infinite—it can be challenged through upward pressure, or weightlessness simulations, and can be overruled once we leave Earth's Exosphere. Similarly, the law about the irreconcilable antagonism between the proletarian and the bourgeoisie (between any exploited and exploiting class) does not close all avenues to change and movement within the system. For example, infighting occurs within each class, and sometimes sectors of either classes unite in temporary, strategic alliances.

A second misconception about historical materialism is that it presents a stageist view of history. They say the steps from feudalism to capitalism to socialism to communism are laid out in a predetermined order. However, in one of his critiques of Hegel, the *Grundrisse*, Marx dismisses the Hegelian temporal rule that "the latest form regards the previous ones as steps leading up to itself."[41] Hegel said that the current historical stage always views the stage before it as a step leading up to itself, as if on a ladder. Marx explains that he views the process differently. He in fact provided a biological example to make the point. He wrote that while it is true that "human anatomy contains a key to the anatomy of the ape," this doesn't mean that human anatomy is the teleological outcome of the ape.[42] Teleological in the sense that the goal of the process was already predetermined—that the human was always destined to emerge from the ape, that capitalism was always destined to come from feudalism. Convinced by Darwinist evolutionary biology, Marx insisted that while *step two* emerges from its *step one*, there is no guarantee about how it will emerge, or if it will ever emerge. A conjunction of intersect-

---

40   Derek Ford, "Marx's inquiry and presentation: The pedagogical constellations of the Grundrisse and Capital," *Educational Philosophy and Theory* 54, no.11 (2022): 35.

41   Karl Marx and M Nicolaus, *Grundrisse: Foundations of the Critique of Political Economy (Rough Draft)* (New York: Penguin Books and New Left Review, 1939), 106.

42   Ibid., 105.

ing factors, of accumulated contradictions, including human agency, will have to determine its final form. Althusser rightly suggested that "Marx would say: every result is plainly the result of a becoming, but its becoming does not contain that result in itself."[43] The result is still a product of struggle and chance, while also being a product of what it came from. Biodigital concepts such as the genetic evolution of the human species have been used by Marxists (including Marx) to gain a deeper understanding of our method. Thus given that the challenges we face in the current day are deeply biological, and that historical materialism is biodigital in methodological form, this is a surprisingly fitting philosophical method.

Conclusion

In a neglected sentence in *A Contribution to the Critique of Political Economy*, Marx says that his conclusion is nothing more than a new beginning that "once reached, continued to serve as the leading thread in my studies."[44] That Marx views his conclusions as another starting point of study demonstrates a particular historical-materialist pedagogy that neither disavows politics nor is determined solely by the class struggle. It demonstrates the permanent openness of the method when it comes to the class struggle. It also demonstrates a biological and reproductive ethic where the end of a life is nothing but the beginning of a new one. All decay gives life, whether the rotting carcass enriches the forest soil, or new babies are born to fill the absence of the passing elderly.

This conclusion hopes, similarly, to return the reader to a new beginning. I began this essay with the wager that historical materialism and postdigital research could be fellow travelers, companions even. Over the course of the pages, the two have overlapped, helped each other out; they have become one, diverged, drifted apart, and gone their separate ways. In our historical moment, the working people of the world are suffering acutely, to different degrees, at the hands of the same system. At such a time, we cannot be satisfied with critique alone. We must also

---

43   Louis Althusser, *History and imperialism: Writings, 1963–1986*, ed. and trans. G. M. Goshgarian (Cambridge: Polity Press): 149.

44   Marx, *A Contribution to the Critique of Political Economy* (1859/1904), 11.

build theoretical apparatuses that can give us hope for a better world system. We must combine tools found in disparate theoretical approaches to build a united research front that can take on the postdigital challenges in front of us. It is with this sense of urgency, that I offer historical materialism as a postdigital method of philosophy.

CHAPTER 7
UNITING THE DIVIDED CONCEPT OF THE UNITED FRONT: A BRIEF HISTORY

Nicholas Stender

NICHOLAS STENDER is a writer, activist, and working class organizer. He works as a public school educator and is a member of his local union.

TECTONIC SHIFTS IN WORLD POWER are shifting the political landscape. The imperialist world system is fraying at the seams as more and more countries ditch the dollar trading system. Climate catastrophe looms like a specter over our collective future. Automation and AI threaten to eliminate millions of jobs. All of these interconnected crises affect the consciousness of the masses of people. In the United States, 54% of people aged 18 to 34 believe socialism will improve the economy and well-being of citizens.[1] Since 2016, legions of young people have started to identify as socialist. The popularity of unions is at near record highs[2] and working class consciousness is increasing, as exemplified by the successful contract struggle of the Teamsters against UPS.[3]

Many new participants in these social movements are radical and want to see a higher degree of unity among working people as a whole. This represents an elementary understanding that the ultimate victory of the working class requires unity, but what exactly *is it*?

Since its introduction into the communist movement in 1922, the political formula of the United Front has been the answer to the ques-

---

1   Savage, "Even Right-Wing Think Tanks Are Finding High Support for Socialism."

2   Marino, "Union Popularity Hits 57-Year High."

3   Horstmann, "How We Beat the Company."

tion, "What is working class unity?" Ironically, there hasn't always been much agreement on the fundamentals of this concept. Many different parties, tendencies, figures, and movements have adopted or invoked the formula of the United Front to explain their strategy for the revolutionary movement.[4] The variety of interpretations of the United Front formula has also implied contradictory forms of political practice. When one talks about "building a United Front" what do they mean? What is the difference between a United Front and coalitions of allies? Is unity when everyone just gets along?

The conditions that gave birth to the United Front formula are similar in a number of ways to conditions facing the working class today. Imperialist powers menace the socialist camp. The capitalist class is undertaking a major assault on the rights and living conditions of the working class. Fascism is on the rise throughout imperialist countries. Capitalist democracy is losing its legitimacy in the eyes of many, yet the majority of workers still hold out hopes in reformist politics or are politically inactive. Many communist parties in imperialist countries are often small, relatively new, or untested. Contradictions within the world economic and political system are maturing, with major crises on the horizon. An analysis of the United Front period can help class conscious workers learn from the debates of the past and develop a synthesis to meet the challenges of our times.

This essay provides a historical grounding of the United Front formula, examines the theoretical basis of the United Front, and outlines some of the enduring questions posed by the United Front policy.

The United Front was formulated after a prolonged period that encompassed the decomposition of the 2nd International and the refoundation of the socialist movement into the 3rd International. From the fall of the Paris Commune in 1871 to the beginning of WWI in 1914, European social democratic parties expanded their reach into the working class by building a large trade union apparatus and mass parties that encompassed the vast majority of the working class. This prolonged period of slow expansion and lack of revolutionary explosions, notwithstanding the 1905 Russian Revolution, led to the spread of reformist illusions

---

4   Examples of the varying interpretations of the formula can be seen in Del Roio, *The Prisms of Gramsci: Political Formula of the United Front*, 69–70.

within these parties. The contradiction between the stated goals of these social democratic parties and their actual actions came to a head at the start of WWI. In contradiction to the 1912 Basel Declaration,[5] which called on social democrats to use the occasion of war to overthrow the capitalist class, social democratic representatives voted to support their own capitalist classes and finance WWI.

This betrayal by social democratic leaders led to a debate between different wings of the socialist movement around the nature of social democracy, and thereby the question of whether any unity could be found with the reformist social democrats who supported the war. The debate is best exemplified in an exchange surrounding the famous Junius pamphlet written by Polish-German revolutionary Rosa Luxemburg in 1915.[6] For socialists, internationalists, and opponents of WWI, the Junius pamphlet rang out like a clarion call for class struggle to end the imperialist war. Despite the enthusiasm generated by the strong critique of the war, Luxemburg could not identify the social roots of the split within social democracy.

Lenin argued that, "[t]he chief defect in [Luxemburg's] pamphlet [...] is its silence regarding the connection between social-chauvinism (the author uses neither this nor the less precise term social-patriotism) and opportunism."[7] Luxemburg's argument didn't touch on the fact that, "in the epoch of imperialism, owing to objective causes [i.e. super exploitation of the colonies], the proletariat has been split into two international camps, one of which has been corrupted by the crumbs that fall from the table of the dominant-nation bourgeoisie—obtained, among other things, from the double or triple exploitation of small nations."[8] In practice, Luxemburg's policy refused to split the revolutionary left from the Social Democratic Party of Germany (SPD) because she could not see that the party's class base was rooted in its own internal bureaucracy, trade union bureaucracy, and a fraction of well-paid union workers, which Engels called the labor aristocracy. These class strata identified less with the oppressed working class itself and more with the capitalists

---

5   "Manifesto of the International Socialist Congress at Basel."

6   Luxemburg, "The Junius Pamphlet."

7   Lenin, "The Junius Pamphlet."

8   Lenin, "The Discussion On Self-Determination Summed Up."

and petit-bourgeois elements with whom they rubbed shoulders. Lenin wrote, "[Luxemburg] has not completely rid [herself] of the 'environment' of the German Social-Democrats, even the Lefts, who are afraid of a split, who are afraid to follow revolutionary slogans to their logical conclusions."[9]

One of the fatal mistakes of the German revolutionaries was the lack of attention and effort put into building a revolutionary party completely independent of the social democrats. At the time of the revolutionary crisis of November 1918, the Left-wing revolutionary socialists did not organize into an independent, highly disciplined vanguard party but were in a heterogeneous electoral and political bloc with anti-war social democrats. This party was called the Independent Social Democratic Party (USPD) and was composed of a wide variety of political views, with a pro-social democratic right wing and a revolutionary socialist left wing. The one unifying principle of this grouping was the fact that the basis of unity within this political bloc was the call to put an end to WWI.

When the final offensive of the German military failed in 1918, a mutiny among the sailors spiraled into a massive uprising of soldiers and workers. The king was forced to abdicate and a republic was proclaimed. The USPD and the SPD ended up being the two largest parties in Germany. Revolution brought confusion. Who was in charge? In this rapidly shifting environment workers' councils were formed through the spontaneous action of millions who were inspired by the Bolshevik Revolution of 1917.

The workers' councils represented the seeds of the future socialist state. These seeds needed to be nurtured. Unfortunately, many workers didn't understand the significance of the councils and couldn't see just how hostile the SPD and capitalist forces were to them. To strangle the councils and cement the power of the capitalists, the SPD paid lip service to the power of the councils while preparing to call a Constituent Assembly that would form a new constitution on a capitalist basis. This constitution was designed to eliminate the workers' councils and put off any talk of transitioning to socialism.

---

9   Lenin, "The Junius Pamphlet."

Competing trends of socialists and social democrats attempted to lead the councils. By allying themselves with the army, capitalists, and middle classes, the SPD was able to outmaneuver the USPD who were hamstrung by the many incoherencies within their bloc. Time and again, the right wing of the USPD sabotaged the left wing revolutionaries. By the time the Left freed itself from the USPD and formed the Communist Party of Germany (KPD), it was too late. Without the required organizational and political preparation, the young party launched a half-hearted attempt to seize power in January 1919. Their goal was to strengthen the workers' councils and prevent the organization of the capitalist-supported parliament. The SPD had long before begun preparations to organize the Freikorps, an ultra-right militia financed by the capitalists and formed out of demobilized and disoriented soldiers. This counter-revolutionary militia was thrown at the armed workers in January. Despite heroic resistance, the leaders of the KPD were murdered, the councils dismantled, and workers disarmed.

Historian Pierre Broué sums up the errors of the revolutionary Leftists in this period:

The drama and historic weakness of the German workers' and soldiers' councils is ultimately bound up with the fact that there did not exist a real "conciliar party," to encourage and invigorate them, and to take part in the struggle for conciliar power, which the Bolsheviks were able to do between February and October 1917. On the decisive problem of 'constituent assembly or councils,' the leaders of the right wing of the USPD [...] adopted, with a few fine differences, the positions of the SPD [...] This confusion and the absence of a revolutionary organization to lead a consistent struggle for winning the majority in the councils and for the seizure of state power by the councils, left the field clear for the enemies of the councils who were at work within them.[10]

The experience of Germany in the 1918-1919 Revolution proved that a revolution would not be possible without the organizational independence of the class conscious vanguard of the working class. German communists' commitment to unity was to the *abstract* unity of "one big party," not the *concrete* unity of a program or united action. This prevented the working class from being able to clearly identify the dif-

---

10 Broué, *The German Revolution, 1917-1923*, 167.

ferent political lines of the parties at the time. These same errors were not isolated to Germany. In Italy, the revolutionaries' bloc with spineless reformists led to a terrible defeat in the 1919-1920 revolutionary crisis.[11]

The defeats of the post-war revolutions indicated that unprincipled unity within the working class movement, a tendency known as "centrism" was a generalized phenomenon. This tendency required a rectification. As the most prestigious party of the new Communist International, the Bolsheviks set strict membership requirements for the new revolutionary parties who were applying to join *en masse*. The tenor of the requirements is summed up in the document's strongly worded point seven, which stated, "It is the duty of parties wishing to belong to the Communist International to recognize the need for a complete and absolute break with reformism and "Centrist" policy, and to conduct propaganda among the party membership for that break. Without this, a consistent communist policy is impossible. The Communist International demands imperatively and uncompromisingly that this break be effected at the earliest possible date."[12]

Lenin's *Terms of Admission* introduced what researcher Marcos Del Roio calls, "a theoretico-political scission as the foundation for the communist movement, contributing to division among the socio-political forces of the working class."[13] If revolutionaries were going to join the Communist International, they had to form their own independent parties. One can see the seriousness with which the communists undertook this scission and their persistent attempts to consolidate the break with reformism in the minutes on the French question of the 1922 Fourth Congress of the Communist International, during which Trotsky remarked, "We demand of you [the French Communist Party] only that you break once and for all with your former conduct, your former connections [with the social-democrats], your former relationship with capitalist society and its institutions—and that you do so not merely in form but through your deeds, your ideas, your feelings, and your conduct as a whole."[14]

---

11   Stender, "Antonio Gramsci."
12   Lenin, *On the International Working-Class and Communist Movement*, 332.
13   Del Roio, *The Prisms of Gramsci: Political Formula of the United Front*, 15.
14   Riddell, *Toward the United Front: Proceedings of the Fourth Congress of the Commu-*

Communists recognized and fully embraced a concrete contradiction when they split from the reformists: while the unity of the working class was a precondition for its victory over the capitalists, it was necessary to break that unity to draw a clear line of demarcation between reformists and revolutionaries. This line of demarcation existed not only in theory but also in objective differences within the working class.

One of the contradictions of the capitalist system is that while it centralizes society into two classes, the proletariat and the bourgeoisie, it simultaneously divides these two basic classes into a number of different class strata and intermediate classes. These strata are determined by the division of labor within capitalism and the historical particularities of capitalism's development in different nations. Some of the instantiations of the division of labor include the division between mental and physical labor, the division between town and country, the gendered division between "men's work" and "women's work," and the division between industrial work and service work. Additionally, and perhaps most importantly, capitalism's historical development was also accomplished through a division of the working class into oppressed nations and oppressor nations. All of these divisions had the effect of facilitating the accumulation of capital in the hands of the few, increasing the productivity of labor, breaking the unity of the working class, and increasing the rate of surplus value extraction from workers.

The objective stratification of the working class keeps the working class divided and makes united action against the capitalists difficult. This objective stratification is reflected in the minds of the working class as subjective differentiation. Put another way, people think differently about how to live their lives and structure society due to the different forms of social human life activity they perform on a daily basis. For example, it is likely that a small business owner, whose social human life activity encompasses hiring the labor of workers to make a profit for him, would support a political party that championed "free enterprise" and the ingenuity of "entrepreneurs" instead of one which represented the unity and solidarity of labor. Subjective differentiation manifests in the political sphere by the multiplication of different political parties, splits into different tendencies, and the rendering, under capitalism, of a

---

nist International,1922, 968.

more or less large section of the proletariat politically inert.

In the final analysis, the objective fragmentation within the working class is only overcome by the constitution and reinforcement of the communist party. This party unites the working class not on the basis of narrow sectoral interests but on the basis of a totalizing theory of history and society, directed toward the aim of the total liberation of the working class. But how is this process achieved? At the dawn of a revolutionary period, communists represent a small minority of the working class. This is an organic representation of the process of the uneven and combined development of capitalist social relations as they are imposed on the workers. Under pressure of a crisis and through the activity of a revolutionary party, communist influence among the class grows. This process, however, doesn't happen automatically. The communists' success is predicated on a correct evaluation of the conditions of struggle and the adoption of strategies and tactics that fit the period.

For the period immediately following WWI, the strategy of the Communist International was to force a split within social democratic parties, consolidate the revolutionary elements around an independent revolutionary program, and form communist parties. With the scission completed, new communist parties posed the question: we have broken with the reformists, so what next? What strategies do we adopt for the next period of party building? The new communist parties suffered from several acute ailments. First, the leadership cadres of the communist parties were untested in authentically revolutionary politics. In many cases, key leaders had been killed or imprisoned in the post-war revolutionary wave. In other cases, the leadership was coming out of the stuffy environment of reformist social democratic parties and still learning how to wage class struggle. Second, the new parties were by and large separated from the masses of working class and oppressed people.

Many communists expected the working class to immediately throw the social democratic leaders overboard and come over to the communists during a period of revolution. Despite betrayal after betrayal by the leaders of social democracy, the majority of the working class of Europe and the United States continued to support parties and trade unions allied with these social democratic forces. The enduring support of the working class for social democracy represented a problem for the communists. Why did the working class remain tethered to social democracy despite repeated betrayals and failures? What is the historic role of social democracy and what is the correct policy to take towards social democratic workers and parties?

Many of the young revolutionaries joining communist parties had come to political activity and consciousness in the fierce struggle against reformism and "centrism" inaugurated by the Communist International. It was because of this that they had a somewhat skewed perception of what it meant to be a communist. They were less oriented towards winning the majority of the working class to socialism and revolution and more oriented towards doing battle with the reformists, "centrists," and traitors within the working class movement. They were children of the scission, so to speak, and like all children, they suffered from growing pains. To speed the process of their political development and to impart the hard lessons that the Bolsheviks learned over their many decades of struggle in Russia, Lenin wrote the famous pamphlet, "Left Wing Communism: An Infantile Disorder" prior to the Second Congress of the Communist International in 1920. This pamphlet addressed several major issues within the new international movement.

The first was the misconception that the Bolsheviks were a revolutionary party because in each and every moment they advocated the most revolutionary tactics and slogans. Lenin argued that this commitment to certain tactics *as a principle* was an error of dogmatism when he wrote that, "The Bolsheviks' boycott of "parliament" in 1905 enriched the revolutionary proletariat with highly valuable political experience and showed that, when legal and illegal parliamentary and non-parliamentary forms of struggle are combined, it is sometimes useful and even essential to reject parliamentary forms. It would, however, be highly erroneous to apply this experience blindly, imitatively and uncritically to *other* conditions and *other* situations. The Bolsheviks' boycott of the Duma [Russian parliament] in 1906 was a mistake, although a minor and easily remediable one."[15] While the slogan of rejecting participation in a capitalist parliament sounds revolutionary, there are circumstances where it is the incorrect tactic. Simply choosing the most revolutionary tactic at all times would leave the communists isolated when the masses

---

15 Lenin, *Selected Works*, 3:303.

weren't in a revolutionary mood. The basic lesson in this was that any attempt to find a ready made formula for revolution was doomed to failure. All tactics and strategies must be justified by the particular balance of forces of a concrete situation. An analysis of these forces isn't easy to arrive at. It requires experience, links to the masses, and a strong grasp of history on the part of the leadership. The young communist parties would have to think for themselves.

A second error of the young communists was a commitment to "purity" politics. There was a general conception that communists should be the permanent opposition to the reformists and "centrists", that the best way to do this was to stand apart from existing organizations and institutions, including working class organizations like trade unions with reformist leadership, and attempt to influence them from without. This was the extension of the scission line of the Communist International taken to the extreme. Lenin argued that communists must not make the mistake of confusing the leadership of unions with the membership. He argued that it was necessary to join the working class wherever it could be found and struggle to win them over to the correct line.[16] The party had to utilize all forms of struggle to raise the consciousness and organizational level of the working class. In this conception, the role of communists was reoriented from that of permanent opposition to permanent persuader and educator.

This polemic with the ultra-left injected an element of nuance into the struggle against reformism. Now that the split within the working class movement between the revolutionaries and reformists was complete on the level of parties, the struggle must continue within the organizations of the working class and in the political forums that they looked to for leadership. Communists were asked, without slackening for a moment the ideological fight against reformist illusions, to enter organizations wherever the masses were gathering to organize for a principled line on issues that were of concrete and direct importance to the working class.

This change in emphasis was due to the concrete situation of the early 1920s. It was clear to the Communist International that the postwar revolutionary upsurge spurred by the twin pressures of the Bolshe-

---

16   Lenin, 3:317.

vik revolution and the catastrophic social crisis caused by WWI was giving way to a new period. By 1921 the capitalist class went on the assault against workers' standards of living and organizations, emboldened by the defeats suffered by the proletariat in the postwar revolutionary wave and a stabilization in the world economy which was driven primarily by the expansion of U.S. industry.[17] In this unfavorable international environment, communists could not put out a call to go on the offensive. In fact, when they did so their assaults ended in bitter defeat.

In this context, one of the leaders of the Communist Party of Germany, Paul Levi, came up with an original solution. On behalf of the KPD, he drafted an open letter to all of the reformist parties, trade unions, and workers' organizations across the country.[18] In this letter he outlined the attacks on workers' rights, the declining standards of living, and increasingly violent repression from the capitalist class. He put forward a series of proposals to engage in united action to fight for higher wages, ensure the supply of food, disarm capitalist militias, free political prisoners, a national jobs program, empowerment of working class councils, and more. The open letter was, at its root, a call out: if the reformists call themselves socialists or say they are for the working class, then it is time for them to put their money where their mouth is, set aside differences, and engage in united action to defend the workers. Predictably, the leadership of the reformist parties ignored the letter but workers took to it. The appeal to unity spoke to their immediate needs. Levi didn't attempt to ignore the differences between the reformists and revolutionaries but put the struggle for the concrete needs of workers in the foreground. Even though Levi departed from the communist movement, Lenin was to speak highly of the tactic of the open letter and advocated it as a basis for all communist parties.[19]

The tactic of the open letter was systematized and generalized into the formula of the United Front prior to the Fourth Congress of the Communist International. All communist parties were called on to reach out to the reformists and "centrists" they so recently attacked and

---

17   For an account of the world economic situation at this time, see Riddell, *To The Masses: Proceedings of the Third Congress of the Communist International, 1921*, 102–33.

18   Riddell, 1061–63.

19   Riddell, 1098.

to make an appeal to defend the working class on the same terms as the open letter.

The United Front was different from the so-called unity of the USPD. Instead of dissolving into one big party, the Communist International believed, "that the chief and categorical condition, the same for all Communist Parties, is: the absolute autonomy and complete independence of every Communist Party entering into any agreement with the parties of the Second and Two-and-a-Half Internationals [i.e. the reformist social democrats], and its freedom to present its own views and its criticisms of those who oppose the Communists."[20] Freedom of criticism was designed to maintain the ideological independence of the communists from the reformists. Clearly, the Communists weren't abandoning the task of scission or abandoning a revolutionary perspective but recognized the changing conditions when they wrote, "every serious mass action, even if it starts only with immediate demands, will inevitably place more general and fundamental questions of the revolution on the agenda. The Communist vanguard can only win if new layers of workers become convinced through their own experience that reformism is an illusion and that compromise on policy is fatal."[21] This policy was intended to win over the workers to revolution by separating them from their reformist leadership and creating the ideal conditions in the country for the rapid education of the working class. The struggle is the greatest teacher.

Many activists today are familiar with the concept of a coalition where many diverse organizations or individuals come together to accomplish a task or hold a mass action. The major differences between a United Front and a coalition are the scope of action and the class forces that make up the bloc of forces. To the Communist International, it was possible to envision a situation in which communists might enter into a temporary coalition with capitalist parties—and in this case, the coalition was marked by the communists' readiness to break it up. This happened in the course of the Russian Revolution where the Bolsheviks took up arms to defend the workers and soldiers councils and the

---

20   Riddell, *Toward the United Front: Proceedings of the Fourth Congress of the Communist International,1922*, 1170.

21   Riddell, 1165.

capitalist government of Kerensky against the ultra-right wing coup attempt led by Kornilov.²² They didn't stop for a single moment agitating against the capitalist-led government and after the coup attempt was defeated, the Bolsheviks even offered to support the reformist social-democrats in a United Front if they seized power from the capitalists. The offer, of course, was rejected but this episode demonstrates some of the differences between a coalition and United Front. A coalition represents a short-term coming together of different class forces to achieve concrete aims. A United Front represents a long-term horizon designed to win the support of workers who are confused by reformism by engaging in common action, elevating the level of struggle, and raising the consciousness of the working class.

The United Front policy was one of the most significant achievements of the Communist International. It provided a framework for communists to fortify their parties by demonstrating to the working class the seriousness and discipline of communists in fighting for the survival of workers. In the process, the United Front transformed communist parties from small propaganda groups into large mass parties with serious influence within the working class.

Even though the Fourth Congress of the Communist International formulated the fundamental theses of the United Front and provided concrete direction to parties in different countries on how to consolidate the United Front, the congress did not resolve all of the questions raised by the turn to the new policy. The United Front strategy was not immune to the changing political winds in the Soviet Union.²³ Despite its clear successes, the United Front policy fell victim to the faction fight within the Russian Communist Party, which spilled over into the Communist International. Due to the early death of the United Front, many of the debates surrounding the correct application of the policy remain open to this day, including:

1. Does the United Front open up a possibility for a workers' and peasants' government, composed of a bloc of parties of the working class and peasantry? If communists enter the government through

---

22 Trotsky, "What Next?"
23 Del Roio, *The Prisms of Gramsci: Political Formula of the United Front*, 105.

a United Front do they risk becoming co-opted themselves[24]? How far should communist parties go in forming United Fronts for elections?

2. To what extent should communists use United Front formations to prepare the working class for a revolution and civil war against the capitalists? For example, if a United Front government comes to power should it immediately go about arming the workers to defend against counter-revolution?

3. When is the right time to break a United Front? How should that break be carried out?

4. Is the United Front a phase that all communist parties will have to pass through in one way or another? Or is the United Front only useful for a particular historical period?

5. Is a United Front with capitalist parties possible in defense of democratic rights, say against the threat of fascism?

6. What are the concrete, immediate demands of today that will galvanize and unite the working class into a United Front?

These questions will be resolved by a new generation of communists and working-class militants, rising to the occasion to organize and lead the working class to its final victory.

---

24 For an analysis of this phenomenon, see Marcy, *Eurocommunism: New Form of Reformism*, 15–17.

CHAPTER 8
THEORETICAL AND PRACTICAL SELF-DETERMINATION OF INDIGENOUS NATIONS IN THE SOVIET UNION

Nolan Long

NOLAN LONG is a Canadian undergraduate student in political studies, with a specific interest in Marxist political theory and history.

Introduction: Indigeneity in the Soviet Union

The Union of Soviet Socialist Republics was home to huge swaths of nationalities, including numerous Indigenous nations, many of which were located in Siberia. The Russian Empire, which preceded the Soviet Union, engaged in the systematic oppression of all minority nationalities while promoting Great Russian nationalism.[1] As a result, it was a prime issue for the Bolsheviks to address national woes and relations. The Leninist approach to nationalities enshrined the equality of nations, opposed nationalism, and supported the unconditional right to self-determination. This right bore a special class character; in essence, the working and exploited classes of Indigenous nations gained the right to self-determination, not the ruling classes. The practical policies of the Soviets largely lined up with their theoretical outlying, suggesting good faith on the part of the state towards the Indigenous peoples of the USSR.

One aspect of the Soviet approach to nationalities is that indigeneity, as such, was not expressly considered. While Indigenous nations

---

1   Sidorova, Evgeniia, and Rice, Roberta. "Being Indigenous in an Unlikely Place: Self-Determination in the Yakut Autonomous Soviet Socialist Republic (1920-1991)." p. 5.

were, in some cases, afforded special privileges,² Indigenous groups were firstly seen as minority nationalities, not as Indigenous nationalities. But it was because of the positive Soviet policy toward minority nationalities that Indigenous rights were, in some sense inadvertently, protected. The Soviet approach to national self-determination allowed Indigenous groups in the Soviet Union to flourish and experience a relatively high quality of living and independence, despite the lack of direct recognition of that indigeneity.

Indigenous groups in the Russian SFSR existed primarily in the North and the Far East.³ Under the policy of the Russian Empire, the Indigenous peoples of these lands were negatively affected by the tsarist government. They were subjected to European diseases, resource extraction, settler colonialism, and induced alcoholism.⁴ Contrastingly, the Soviet policy towards Indigenous groups was based on development, socialism, and the right of nations to self-determination. This essay deals with Soviet Indigenous groups generally while occasionally looking at the Yakut for specificity. The Sakha/Yakut are an Indigenous group in Siberia who, during the Soviet era, maintained their ancient cultural practices (such as reindeer breeding) while also industrially developing under Soviet policy.⁵ The Yakut had their own autonomous region, which allowed them to maintain their own culture.⁶ Soviet policy stated that Indigenous groups with a population over 50,000 were to be recognized as ethnic minorities, rather than Indigenous as such.⁷ However, the Indigenous groups with populations over this threshold (including the Yakut) were allowed to assemble into ASSRs with the right to self-determination.⁸ The Soviet approach was complex due to this mutual recognition of the right of nations to self-determination,

---

2   Sulyandziga, Pavel. "We Need Two Keys."

3   Bartels, Davis A., and Bartels, Alice L. *When the North was Red: Aboriginal Education in Soviet Siberia.* p. ix.

4   Ibid., p. 16-22.

5   Ibid., p. x.

6   Ibid., p. 1.

7   Ibid.

8   Ibid.

and the lack of recognition of the status of certain Indigenous groups. This dichotomy necessitates a study into the theoretical policy of the Bolsheviks.

The Theoretical Marxist-Leninist Approach to Nationalities and Self-Determination

In 1914, V.I. Lenin wrote, "self-determination of nations means the political separation of these nations from alien national bodies and the formation of an independent national state."[9] It is undeniable that the Soviet conceptions of nations and self-determination differed significantly from the Western ones.[10] J.V. Stalin added to this definition: "The right to self-determination means that only the nation itself has the right to determine its destiny, that no one has the right forcibly to interfere in the life of that nation, to destroy its schools and other institutions, to violate its habits and customs, to repress its language, or curtail its rights."[11] This conception mapped out the later Soviet practice, which allowed for the political independence of Finland and the Baltic states shortly after the Russian Revolution, even while the Western nations opposed Soviet support for self-determination.[12]

Western opposition to the self-determination of nations, in the Soviet sense, was opposition to the emancipation of Indigenous and minority nations from tsarist rule, as well as opposition to socialist sovereignty. Gerald Taiaiake Alfred argues that the Western model of sovereignty is incompatible with Indigenous governance methods/structures. Indigenous governance is traditionally without absolute authority, hierarchy, or classism.[13] In comparison, the Soviet model of sovereignty, derived from its theory of nations and the right to self-determination, seems to be more compatible with Indigenous society and governance,

---

9   Lenin, V.I. *The Right of Nations to Self-Determination.* p. 4.

10   Goshulak, Glenn. "Soviet and Post-Soviet Challenges to the Study of Nation and State Building." p. 494.

11   Stalin, J.V. *Marxism and the National and Colonial Question.* p. 18.

12   Anderson, Edgar. "Finnish-Baltic Relations, 1918-1940." p. 52.

13   Alfred, Gerald Taiaiake. "'Sovereignty': An Inappropriate Concept." p. 323.

given its tendency towards class abolition.

But while Finland, the Baltic states, and others gained their independence on the basis of Soviet support for self-determination, none of the many Indigenous nations did. Whether this is because the Bolsheviks opposed the rights of Indigenous nations to secession, or because these nations did not want to secede, is undeniably a debated topic. However, the evidence seems to show that Indigenous groups (at least their previously exploited classes) supported the new government. For example, communists were at work in the Yakutia working class and peasantry.[14] So, while they did not become independent, the Indigenous nations generally seem to have been in support of the new Russian Soviet Socialist state nonetheless.

The Leninist approach recognized the necessity of nations to be able to pursue their own paths of development and to protect their own cultures. This doctrine was derived from two related sources: fighting Great Russian nationalism[15] and adhering to proletarian internationalism.[16] Great Russian nationalism was that of the dominating nationality, of the ruling class of the Russian Empire. As the Bolsheviks believed in the equality of nations,[17] they believed in the necessity of fighting this nationalism in tandem with their struggle against Russian tsarism and capitalism. Proletarian internationalism is the belief that the working classes of all nations should share a sense of brotherhood in their mutual struggles against their respective ruling classes. Resultantly, Lenin believed it was in the interests of the Great Russian proletariat to struggle against the oppression that their bourgeoisie imposed upon minority nations.[18] "The Leninist position is made up of two intersecting tendencies: an internationalist outlook, and a support for the right to self-determination."[19]

---

14 Kirby, Stuart E. "Communism in Yakutia—The First Decade." p. 29.

15 Lenin, V.I. *The Right of Nations to Self-Determination.* p. 48.

16 Ibid., p. 91.

17 Stalin, J.V. *Marxism and the National and Colonial Question.* p. 18.

18 Lenin, V.I. *The Right of Nations to Self-Determination.* p. 31.

19 Bedford, David. "Marxism and the Aboriginal Question: The Tragedy of Progress." p. 108.

The Bolshevik leaders said relatively little about indigeneity. Rather, they focused on the "national question," and thus viewed Indigenous nations as minority nationalities in most cases. Consequently, the Soviet Indigenous policy was bound up in the national policy. Lenin did not say whether Indigenous groups should receive special status, but he "asserted the absolute, unconditional right of peoples to self-determination, including secession from a future socialist state."[20] Stalin did not say whether Indigenous groups should receive political independence, but said that *all* minority nationalities (thus inclusive of Indigenous groups) have the right "to arrange its life on the basis of autonomy [...] [and] the right to complete secession."[21] This silence on the question of Indigeneity is at least partially attributable to the fact that the Russian Revolution and the Bolshevik Party existed well before the modern centrality of Indigenous rights and politics on national and global stages. Nonetheless, the Soviet approach to national self-determination allowed indigenous groups in the Soviet Union to experience cultural development and protection, and levels of independence unparalleled in the Western world.

The Question of Class

Both Lenin and Stalin made it clear that the right to self-determination had a class character. Lenin wrote that the proletarian approach to self-determination "supports the bourgeoisie only in a certain direction, but never coincides with the bourgeoisie's policy."[22] The Russian proletariat, he said, should support the right of the oppressed nationalities to form their own state, as this right opposes Great Russian nationalism.[23] Stalin also made it clear that the right to self-determination does not mean that the socialist state should support every aspect of that national independence, at least when its independence puts it under bourgeois rule.[24] Bedford offers a concise summation: "Whether support for the

---

20 Ibid.

21 Stalin, J.V. *Marxism and the National and Colonial Question*. p. 18.

22 Lenin, V.I. *The Right of Nations to Self-Determination*. p. 25-26.

23 Lenin, V.I. *The Right of Nations to Self-Determination*. p. 29-30.

24 Stalin, J.V. *Marxism and the National and Colonial Question*. p. 18.

cultural aspirations of an ethnic group is in effect supporting the Indigenous bourgeoisie against the proletariat, or is serving to further the revolutionary struggle is the definitive question."[25]

The Indigenous nations of the Russian Empire and the Soviet Union did, of course, have class relations, though they were quite different from those of the rest of the country. "Soviet authorities admit that the working class in Yakutia was few in numbers and contained almost no industrial proletariat."[26] The Soviets, thus, had to consider the question of class differently in the Indigenous nations than in the non-Indigenous ones. Firstly, the principle of self-determination had to be analyzed; it was found that the workers and other exploited classes of Indigenous Yakuts were in support of the Russian Revolution.[27] However, the ruling classes of Yakutia, including the kulaks, were "stronger in Yakutia than elsewhere in the Soviet Union."[28] Given these class conditions, the Bolsheviks found that self-determination belonged to the proletariat rather than the bourgeoisie, and aided the exploited Yakut classes in throwing off their ruling classes over a long period of time. Soviet intervention in Yakutia was not based on a policy of eliminating the Indigenous culture, but on removing the bourgeoisie from their culture.

Stalin addressed the question of culture and nationality: "[T]he unity of a nation diminishes [...] owing to the growing acuteness of class struggle."[29] The common culture between the proletariat and bourgeoisie of a nation is weakened by the development of capitalism. This evidences the Bolshevik claim to eliminating bourgeois cultural elements from Indigenous nations while not attacking the culture or people as a whole. For example, Shamans in Yakutia, identified as part of the ruling classes of that nation, were "chastised" as "being responsible for the 'backwardness and ignorance' of Indigenous communities."[30] As

---

25 Bedford, David. "Marxism and the Aboriginal Question: The Tragedy of Progress." p. 109.

26 Kirby, Stuart E. "Communism in Yakutia – The First Decade." p. 29.

27 Ibid.

28 Ibid., p. 39.

29 Stalin, J.V. *Marxism and the National and Colonial Question.* p. 35.

30 Sidorova, Evgeniia, and Rice, Roberta. "Being Indigenous in an Unlikely

such, given the material conditions of the Indigenous nations of the Soviet Union, self-determination took a proletarian character rather than a bourgeois one.

The Reality of Indigenous Self-Determination in the Soviet Union

As previously mentioned, the Soviet government put certain structures in place to ensure the special rights of Indigenous nations/individuals. "For example, if there were regions for hunting or fishing, those territories went to the Indigenous people right away on a natural basis without any constraints."[31] The Committee of the North was a Bolshevik Party organ that "persuaded the Soviet government to extend certain special privileges to northern peoples," including exemption from taxation and conscription.[32] Indeed, while Indigenous groups underwent some degree of change,[33] such as a 'proletarianization,' they were largely allowed to maintain their cultures and regular ways of life. "In the northlands, the indigenous people continued to be nomadic, everywhere the peasants depended largely on hunting and fur-trapping."[34] The Indigenous Dargin people of the Caucasus "preserved their traditional Sufi-influenced Islamic practices and endured less government pressure [to adhere to atheism]."[35]

While the Soviet government attempted to include Indigenous nations in the worker culture of the USSR, their relatively lax approach to Indigenous culture demonstrates some level of good faith. Furthermore, Davis and Alice Bartels argue that "all national and ethnic groups were

---

Place: Self-Determination in the Yakut Autonomous Soviet Socialist Republic (1920-1991)." p. 5.

31   Sulyandziga, Pavel. "We Need Two Keys."

32   Bartels, Davis A., and Bartels, Alice L. *When the North was Red: Aboriginal Education in Soviet Siberia.* p. 30-31.

33   First Peoples Worldwide. "Who are the Indigenous Peoples of Russia?"

34   Kirby, Stuart E. "Communism in Yakutia – The First Decade." p. 36.

35   Eden, Jeff. *God Save the USSR: Soviet Muslims and the Second World War.*

radically changed as a result of Soviet state policy,"[36] not just Indigenous groups. Industrialization, collectivization, educational opening, and the liberation of women were new and radical concepts for both Indigenous and non-Indigenous groups.[37] As such, these policies were not aimed at othering one group, or anything alike. Rather, such policies were aimed at national development and socialist construction.

The Soviets outwardly supported the cultural development and autonomy of Indigenous nations in more explicit ways. "Soviet policy [was] to encourage the development of national cultures and preservation of the native languages."[38] Samir Amin writes that "the Soviet system brought changes for the better. It gave [...] autonomous districts, established over huge territories, the right to their cultural and linguistic expression."[39] This cultural and linguistic expression included "the creation of written forms of [Indigenous] languages and educational programs in northern languages."[40] The Soviet policy towards Indigenous groups was not one of assimilation, but allowance for autonomy (derived from self-determination) in the realm of culture.

Indigenous groups also had political rights which were reflective of their right to self-determination. "Stalin specified that each nationality should man its own courts, administrative bodies, economic agencies and government by its own local native peoples and conduct them in its own language."[41] Lenin likewise argued that it was of great importance to create autonomous regions in Russia.[42] Soviet practice largely lined up with Leninist theory. Directly after the October Revolution, the Bolshevik Party released the Declaration on the Rights of Peoples of Russia,

---

36   Bartels, Davis A., and Bartels, Alice L. *When the North was Red: Aboriginal Education in Soviet Siberia.* p. 4.

37   Ibid.

38   Szymanski, Albert. *Human Rights in the Soviet Union.* p. 51.

39   Amin, Samir. *Russia and the Long Transition from Capitalism to Socialism.* p. 29.

40   Bartels, Davis A., and Bartels, Alice L. *When the North was Red: Aboriginal Education in Soviet Siberia.* p. 5.

41   Ibid., p. 8.

42   Bedford, David. "Marxism and the Aboriginal Question: The Tragedy of Progress." p. 108.

"which guaranteed the right to self-determination and the abolition of religious and ethnic discrimination."[43] Skachko, an academic expert on Siberian Indigenous groups, wrote in 1930 that the Soviet state did not intend to keep Indigenous peoples "as helpless charges of the state in special areas reserved for them and isolated from the rest of the world [...] On the contrary, the government's goal is their all-around cultural and national development and their participation as equals."[44]

Conditions were not perfect for Indigenous nations in the Soviet Union; they experienced some drawbacks as a result of Soviet policies, sometimes due to the lack of recognition of indigeneity. "In 1917, the Yakut/Sakha people constituted 87.1% of the province's total population."[45] However, by the end of the Soviet era, the Indigenous people made up only 33% of the population.[46] Beyond the settlement of Indigenous land by non-Indigenous peoples, another drawback was that traditional Indigenous occupations had been "disrupted by industrial and resource development" by the late 1980s.[47] This is, however, at least partially attributable to the fact that Mikhail Gorbachev was not a Leninist, meaning he did not follow the preceding Soviet approach to nationalities.

The Soviet government "established a system to transfer capital from the rich regions of the Union (western Russia, Ukraine, Belorussia, later the Baltic countries) to the developing regions of the east and south ."[48] By providing aid for the newly autonomous Indigenous republics, the Soviets were expressly supporting their development. Beyond this aid, Indigenous political systems were manned by members of the nation itself. The Soviet policy of *korenization* (nativization) "sought to

---

43   Bartels, Davis A., and Bartels, Alice L. *When the North was Red: Aboriginal Education in Soviet Siberia.* p. 29.

44   Ibid., 30-31.

45   Sidorova, Evgeniia, and Rice, Roberta. "Being Indigenous in an Unlikely Place: Self-Determination in the Yakut Autonomous Soviet Socialist Republic (1920-1991)." p. 7.

46   Ibid., 8.

47   Bartels, Davis A., and Bartels, Alice L. *When the North was Red: Aboriginal Education in Soviet Siberia.* p. xii.

48   Amin, Samir. *Russia and the Long Transition from Capitalism to Socialism.* p. 29.

fill key management positions with Indigenous representatives."⁴⁹ This policy was implemented because "leaders of the governing Bolshevik Party considered Great Russian chauvinism as a major impediment to economic and social development because it turned a blind eye to the national/social aspiration of the many peoples and nationalities in the Soviet Union."⁵⁰ This policy allowed Indigenous nations to develop on their own terms while remaining within the Union, allowing them to express their self-determination without needing to exercise their right to secession.

While it is true that the Indigenous nations did not secede from the Soviet Union, two facts remain that prove that the Soviet state supported the independence of these nations; firstly, these nations were allowed to organize into Autonomous Republics which exercised a large amount of self-governing, even relative to the Soviet state and the Republic states.⁵¹ Second, these nations still (at least theoretically) had the *right* to self-determination.⁵² It is arguable, then, that the Indigenous nations of the USSR merely never exercised the right to cessation due to their support for the Soviet system/government.

Conclusion

In the capitalist Russian Federation, Indigenous peoples are significantly worse off than under the USSR. Russia has not yet adopted the United Nations Declaration on the Rights of Indigenous Peoples,⁵³ nor the ILO Convention 169.⁵⁴ Contrastingly, the Soviet Union was often at the

---

49   Sidorova, Evgeniia, and Rice, Roberta. "Being Indigenous in an Unlikely Place: Self-Determination in the Yakut Autonomous Soviet Socialist Republic (1920-1991)." p. 6.

50   Kovalevich, Dmitri. "Ukrainian Nationalists Have a Long History of Anti-Semitism which the Soviet Union Tried to Combat."

51   Russian Federation's Constitution of 1918. Art. 11.

52   Russian Federation's Constitution of 1918. Art. 6.

53   Representatives of the Republic of Sakha. "An Appeal from the Representatives of the Republic of Sakha (Yakutia) to the United Nations Office of the High Commissioner for Human Rights (OHCHR)."

54   First Peoples Worldwide. "Who are the Indigenous Peoples of Russia?"

forefront of international efforts to recognize Indigenous-centred issues, including the push to recognize cultural genocide in UN documents.[55] While Indigenous groups are formally protected by the Russian Constitution, the enforcement of these protections is often inadequate, leaving these groups in a precarious position where unemployment and poverty rates are high.[56] Whereas the Soviets funded the education of Indigenous languages, the Russian Federation now funds Russian-language schools in these regions, seriously threatening Indigenous languages.[57] Especially in view of the experiences of Indigenous peoples in the modern Russian Federation, the Soviet policies towards Indigenous nations continue to be vindicated.

In their theoretical and practical approaches, the Soviet state was relatively open, egalitarian, and accommodating to the Indigenous groups that lived within its borders. Relative at least to the Western nations, the Soviet Union, existing only until 1991, was consistently measured ahead in its policies towards indigeneity.[58] While not explicitly recognizing the concept of indigeneity in all Soviet Indigenous groups, the state nonetheless provided them with sufficient autonomy for their cultures to be preserved and developed. While imperfect, the Soviet approach was admirable in its own time, to say the very least.

---

55 Mako, Shramiran. "Cultural Genocide and Key International Instruments: Framing the Indigenous Experience." p. 183.

56 First Peoples Worldwide. "Who are the Indigenous Peoples of Russia?"

57 First Peoples Worldwide. "Who are the Indigenous Peoples of Russia?"

58 Szymanski, Albert. *Human Rights in the Soviet Union*. p. 295-296.

CHAPTER 9
CORNEL WEST, THE PITFALLS OF BOURGEOIS POLITICS, AND FORGING A NEW FUTURE AMONG THE RUBBLE

Colin Jenkins

COLIN JENKINS is founding editor of the *Hampton Institute*. His work has been featured in *Black Agenda Report, Truthout, Truthdig, Monthly Review, Counterpunch, Transnational Institute, Z Magazine, Dissident Voice, Popular Resistance*, and other people's media outlets. They've also published in *Social Justice: A Journal of Crime, Conflict, and World Order*, among other places.

ON MONDAY, June 5th, 2023, Cornel West announced his bid to run for the presidency of the United States in 2024. Coming on the heels of two such runs by Bernie Sanders, as well as current runs by Marianne Williamson and Robert Kennedy, Jr. West is seeking to fill what many view as a "progressive" void on the US electoral stage. However, in contrast to the other three, West, a longtime member of the Democratic Socialists of America (DSA), will shun the Democratic Party and run on a third-party ticket under the People's Party.[1]

West's announcement came via his Twitter account, where he has one million followers, and has amassed over 18M views, 47K likes, and 18K shares in a few days. The announcement coincided with an interview on Russell Brand's Rumble livestream, *Stay Free*, and sparked a flurry of mainstream news reports over the last few days.

---

1   **Publisher's Note:** This essay was written prior to the 2024 US presidential election, and prior to Cornel West's presidential run with the Justice For All (JFA) party—a party West co-founded after his withdrawal from the People's Party ticket. We have chosen to retain the tense in which the chapter was written, given the historical and political importance of the questions the author raises with regard to radical electoral strategy in the United States.

We should ask ourselves a few questions. What does this candidacy mean for working-class politics? Considering the recent betrayals by Bernie Sanders, can we expect anything different from West? Can any significant change come from participating in bourgeois elections? And, finally, should working-class people invest time, energy, and resources to support West?

What Does this Mean for Working-Class Politics?

While West's candidacy could properly be described as the most potentially-overt, working-class (that is, anti-capitalist, left-wing) endeavor we have seen on this stage since perhaps the 1960s, it remains to be seen how far he is willing to go. Outside of the Green Party, which has made strides to fill this void in recent years by including explicitly anti-capitalist wording in its national platform and running candidates such as Ajamu Baraka, there is no actual, organized, mainstream left in the United States. Socialist parties that are grounded in working-class emancipation exist, but they are typically small, fragmented, at constant war with one another, and subjected to mainstream censorship. The Green Party itself falls into the same traps, is scattered, and unorganized due to a lack of resources, and has been chronically hamstrung by the capitalist duopoly's (Democrats and Republicans) increasingly difficult standards for ballot representation.

A major problem for authentic working-class politics in the US is the widespread misconception that Democrats and liberals are, in fact, "left-wing." This is an ahistorical belief that is ignorant to the formation, and subsequent historical developments, of political ideology. It is also an issue that has been historically unique to the US, as an international powerhouse birthed from the fascistic wombs of Native Genocide and chattel slavery and maintained by fascist tendencies embedded within the utter dominance of capital (the wealthy minority) over labor (the working majority). It goes without saying that the US government, in serving global capital, has thrived on exploiting not only much of the world, especially the Global South, vis-à-vis colonialism and imperialism, but also much of its own population, especially working-class peoples from historically marginalized demographics (black, brown, women, migrants).

Thus, the country's proclaimed "democracy," or "republic," has never actually been democratic in any genuine manner because self-determination and self-governance do not, and cannot, exist under capitalist modes of production. A "common good" can also not exist, which means that a so-called "social contract" cannot exist. These are realities that were firmly understood by the founders of the country, all of whom were privileged men of wealth hell-bent on breaking free from the confines of a monarchy while simultaneously arranging their own elaborate system of class dominance for centuries to come. The masses have been led to believe that the two capitalist/imperialist political parties that run the US exist in vastly different ideological wings and that we have civic empowerment through the act of voting. However, this could not be further from the truth. A West candidacy has the potential to destroy this illusion simply by showing the people what a genuine working-class (that is, left-wing) candidate looks like—something most have never seen.

However, before we decide on where to stand with West's campaign, there are many questions that need to be pondered: because West's track record is an incredibly mixed bag. There are aspects of his politics that are promising, just as there are aspects that are problematic. In light of the last few elections, we cannot help but ask ourselves if he will choose the same path as Bernie Sanders by building potentially radical momentum among the masses, only to pull the plug and herd us back toward the Democrats. Or will he understand the importance of truly breaking from not only the capitalist duopoly, but also the dominant bourgeois (capitalist) institutions, narratives, and psychological tactics that have us all trapped in a tightly manicured ideological space, inundated with delusions, paranoia, and hysteria pushed by capitalist media? Will he use this campaign in an ironically masterful manner to steer us away from the electoral arena? And, if so, might he leave us with at least a foundation of working-class organizations prepared for the fascist wave, the demise of capitalism, and the United States as we know it?

The Bernie Lesson, the Good and the Bad of West, and Will We Ultimately Be Sold Out Again?

So, will West and his campaign ultimately herd us back to the Democratic Party? Anyone who has been involved in working-class politics—most notably, the Bernie Sanders campaigns—would likely ponder this question with fear, and understandably so. Sanders has been the closest thing we have had as a representative of the working class on a national stage in decades. Sanders' first run in 2016 was especially electric in this regard, as he railed against capitalist greed, did not shy away from the "socialist" label, and generally maintained a solid campaign in support of the working-class masses, at least by US political standards. In terms of tangible results, Sanders spearheaded a formidable organizational following and gave millions of young adults the courage to call themselves "socialists," even if perhaps many still did not know what this meant.

However, as beneficial as Sanders was to many, some noticed warning signs early. As the Sanders phenomenon began to gain steam, the late Bruce Dixon published a scathing critique, and what would come to be a prophetic warning, about Sanders serving as a "sheepdog" for the Democratic Party and its anointed candidate, Hillary Clinton. Unfazed by the momentum, Dixon brilliantly noted:

Spoiler alert: we have seen the Bernie Sanders show before, and we know exactly how it ends. Bernie has zero likelihood of winning the Democratic nomination for president over Hillary Clinton. Bernie will lose, Hillary will win. When Bernie folds his tent in the summer of 2016, the money, the hopes and prayers, the year of activist zeal that folks put behind Bernie Sanders' either vanishes into thin air, or directly benefits the Hillary Clinton campaign.[2]

Dixon's article was labeled as unnecessarily cynical by many at the time. However, to those who had followed electoral politics from a working-class perspective for some time, it was an accurate reflection of a decades-old tactic used by Democrats:

1984 and 88 the sheepdog candidate was Jesse Jackson. In 92 it

---

2   Bruce A. Dixon, "Presidential Candidate Bernie Sanders: Sheepdogging for Hillary and the Democrats in 2016," *Black Agenda Report*, 07 May 2015. Available here: https://www.blackagendareport.com/bernie-sanders-sheepdog-4-hillary.

was California governor Jerry Brown. In 2000 and 2004 the designated sheepdog was Al Sharpton, and in 2008 it was Dennis Kucinich. This year it's Vermont Senator Bernie Sanders. The function of the sheepdog candidate is to give left activists and voters a reason, however illusory, to believe there's a place of influence for them inside the Democratic party, if and only if the eventual Democratic nominee can win in November.[3]

In the end, Dixon's warnings and predictions came to fruition. Sanders did, in fact, throw in the towel, publicly lauded Clinton, and asked his army of loyal followers to support her in the general election against Trump.

A much greater degree of skepticism followed Sanders' second run in 2020. In a 2019 piece for *Left Voice*, Doug Greene exposed Sanders as a consistent supporter of US imperialism, opening with the following breakdown:

> On February 19, 2019, Vermont Senator and "democratic socialist" Bernie Sanders announced his plans to run for the Democratic Party nomination for President. The announcement was met with cheers from large swaths of the American left who identify with his support for expanded labor rights, Medicare for All, free college, and a litany of other progressive issues. Those appear to be very compelling reasons to back the Sanders' campaign. However, when it comes to American imperialism and war, Sanders may offer slightly different rhetoric than other Democratic candidates or Donald Trump, but his record proves him to be no alternative at all.[4]

Greene went on to provide detailed examples of Sanders' support of the US war machine as a battering ram for global capital, which included backing the arms industry during the Reagan years, supporting sanctions and bombings during the Clinton years, supporting Bush's initial response to the 9/11 attacks on the world trade center, providing lukewarm responses to Israel's brutalization of Palestinians while refusing to support the BDS movement, and finally:

---

3   Ibid.

4   Doug Enaa Greene, "Not on Our Side: On Bernie Sanders and Imperialism," *Left Voice*, 18 June 2019. Available here: https://www.leftvoice.org/not-on-our-side-on-bernie-sanders-and-imperialism.

by voting in favor of the military budget in 2009, 2010, and 2013, [...] supporting Obama's military actions against Libya, sanctions against Russia, providing a billion dollars in aid to the far right Ukrainian government in 2014, and support[ing] arming the Saudi Arabian monarchy to fight ISIS.[5]

Ultimately, despite being slighted by the Democrats, which pulled every backdoor maneuver possible to push their corporate candidate, Joe Biden, to the forefront, Sanders once again willingly stepped back, publicly proclaimed Biden to be worthy of the office, and asked everyone to support Biden. While Sanders had already lost a significant amount of support after his first betrayal, this second act of treachery seemed to be the final nail in his coffin. Now, in retrospect, it is difficult for many of even his loyalist followers to see Sanders as anything other than what Bruce Dixon labeled him—a sheepdog who stole the immense time, energy, and resources that he received from millions and handed it over to the capitalist/imperialist Democratic Party, with no strings attached.

Which now brings us to Cornel West, who happened to be a vocal supporter of Sanders. To be fair, Marianne Williamson or Robert Kennedy, Jr. fit the profile of a "sheepdog candidate" much more so than West does. West offers us much greater potential in terms of constructing an authentic, working-class campaign. But, still, we must ask ourselves: is he any different than Sanders?

In many ways, he is. First and foremost, West is not a career Senator of the US imperialist state and a direct surrogate of the Democratic Party. While West supported Sanders during the runups to both presidential elections, he ultimately had the integrity to "disobey" him by endorsing Green Party candidate, Jill Stein, in the 2016 general election. And while West, like many others, threw all of his weight behind the political ascendency of Barack Obama in 2008, he showed bravery and consistency by reconsidering this support shortly after Obama took office, publicly criticizing the country's first black president for his Wall Street appointments, rampant drone strikes, record deportations, and unwillingness to take action for the struggling working-class masses, including the millions of black USAmericans who experienced no tangible benefits from the administration.[6] In doing so, West faced a harsh backlash

---

5   Ibid.

6   Cornel West, "Cornel West Reconsiders President Obama," *NPR*, 02 Au-

from much of the black community, who were understandably high on the symbolic victory and immense significance of seeing a black man in the Oval Office. Many viewed West's criticisms of Obama as "petty jealousy," despite the fact that they were perfectly consistent with West's track record and represented a level of intellectual honesty that is rare in these times.[7]

West has also remained steadfast in his support of the Palestinian people against the apartheid regime in Israel, something that typically amounts to political suicide in the United States (see the recent example of Robert Kennedy, Jr. quickly changing his tune on this very matter when pressured). And perhaps the most important difference is West's willingness to shun the Democratic Party and run as a third-party candidate under the People's Party. There has been much to say about why West chose this relatively unknown party over the seemingly obvious choice of the Green Party, and that may be worthy of investigation, but the importance of this decision is more so in the blatant rejection of the Democrats, who have maintained a decades-long stranglehold on progressives, much of the working class, a large majority of the black community, and even some socialists, despite ongoing militarism, pro-corporate policies, and covert racism.

West has, in many regards, openly pushed for internationalism and has provided a more nuanced opinion on the situation between Russia and Ukraine, ultimately placing much of the blame on the United States and NATO, while calling for the disbandment of NATO.[8] It is difficult to imagine someone like Bernie Sanders, a career Senator of the very state responsible for much of the strife in that region, thinking such

---

gust 2010. Available here: https://www.npr.org/templates/story/story.php?storyId=128933353; Colin Jenkins, " Political Crossover: The Troubling Emergence of 'Black Reaganism,' *Black Agenda Report*, 26 June 2013. Available here: https://www.blackagendareport.com/content/political-crossover-troubling-emergence-black-reaganism.

7   Nsenga Burton, "Cornel West: The Fallout Continues Over Obama Comments," *The Root*, 24 May 2011. Available here: https://www.theroot.com/cornel-west-the-fallout-continues-over-obama-comments-1790864097.

8   Isabel van Brugen, "What 2024 Hopeful Cornel West Has Said About Ukraine," *Newsweek*, 26 June 2023. Available here: https://www.newsweek.com/cornel-west-2024-presidential-bid-peoples-party-ukraine-russia-war-1804730.

things, much less saying them out loud. In fact, Sanders notably hopped on the "Russiagate" train following the 2016 election and has toed the Democratic party line since then.

However, in many ways, West is not different. In 2020, West joined other public intellectuals in supporting Biden as the "anti-fascist choice" in the general election against Trump, essentially going against his consistent opposition of both capitalist parties under the impression that Trump represented the greater threat. West described the battle between the two parties as "catastrophe (Trump and Republicans)" versus "disaster (Biden and Democrats)" and, while noting that Biden was not his first choice, ultimately proclaimed that "catastrophes are worse than disasters" in his official endorsement of Biden:

"There is a difference in neofascist catastrophe and neoliberal disaster," he said. "Catastrophes are worse than disasters. Disasters have less scope and range regarding certain kinds of issues. I never want to downplay the least vulnerable in our society—our gay brothers, lesbian sisters, trans, Black poor, brown poor, Indigenous poor. They are more viciously attacked by the neofascists than the neoliberals. But the neoliberals capitulate to the attack. I would never say they're identical, but I would say poor and working people are still getting crushed over and over again."[9]

On a Facebook post made on September 4, 2020, West shared a video link of his speech along with the explanation that "an anti-fascist vote for Biden is in no way an affirmation of neoliberal politics. In this sense, I agree with my brothers and sisters like Noam Chomsky, Angela Davis, Paul Street, and Bob Avakian." Fifteen months earlier, however, in a Fox News appearance on The Ingraham Angle, West correctly referred to Biden as a "dyed-in-the-wool, backward-looking neoliberal with little vision and even less courage" who "represents a past that hurt black people."

West's attempts to be a unifying force throughout his role as a

---

9   Cornel West, "The Choice is Between 'Disaster' and 'Catastrophe:' The Bottom Line," *Al Jazeera*, 03 September 2020. Available here: https://www.hks.harvard.edu/centers/mrcbg/programs/growthpolicy/choice-between-disaster-and-catastrophe-bottom-line-cornel-west.

public intellectual have led him to appear on platforms that many view as problematic, especially in a time when overt fascism is converging around various forms of bigotry, including *Fox News*, Joe Rogan's podcast, *Real Time* with Bill Maher, and Gavin McInnes'—founder of the Proud Boys—show, to name a few. There are also questions regarding the new People's Party itself, which has faced criticisms about its ineffective organizing and willingness to include and organize right-wing populists towards big-tent efforts. This approach has led to internal strife, rooted mainly in race dynamics, where some black members have felt uneasy about the inclusion of working-class whites who exhibit racist and xenophobic undertones. It is unclear how substantial this problem is within the party but, at a time when identity politics has largely overshadowed and obstructed working-class unity, it is safe to assume that it is significant.

West has openly supported the American Descendants of Slavery (ADOS) movement, which may not seem problematic on the surface, as the call for reparations for black descendants of US slavery is a righteous and worthy cause. But, in doing so, West has ignored a perceived betrayal of Pan-African principles by the organization, which excludes most of the African diaspora throughout the world to embrace a peculiarly pro-US orientation. In a nuanced critique of the organization, Broderick Dunlap tells us:

> There is no question that Black folks in the United States are entitled to reparations for slavery, Jim Crow, mass incarceration, and centuries of racist violence. There is also no question that the United States has caused insurmountable harm to Africans outside of the US. To deny that is to deny history and reality. Understanding that the demand for reparations is an attempt to hold America accountable for harm done to Black folks, excluding Black folks from the conversation contradicts what ADOS claims to be trying to achieve. Besides the impracticality of trying to distinguish between people who are deemed ADOS and other diasporic Africans and biracial Black folks, Africans are socialized and racialized the same as Black folks born in the US. This contradiction is the primary reason it would serve ADOS leaders to adopt Black internationalist principles, so they can build a movement "informed by and engaged with real-world struggles."[10]

Perhaps the most problematic aspect of West's politics, though, has

---

10 Broderick Dunlap, "A Dose of Reality for the #ADOS Movement," *Hood Communist*, 29 April 2021. Available here: https://hoodcommunist.org/2021/04/29/a-dose-of-reality-for-the-ados-movement.

been his willingness to express anti-communist talking points. This willingness stems from the Red Scare era of US history, when anyone and everyone who merely "sympathized" with socialism and communism was ostracized, exiled, imprisoned, and even murdered by the US government. And while such fears have certainly dissipated since the end of the Cold War and the disbandment of the USSR, public intellectuals with large platforms and tenures at major universities are seemingly still held to this standard, with Noam Chomsky being the most notable of this bunch.

West's longtime association with Michael Harrington's DSA also represents an in-between, anti-communist position between capitalism and socialism that is often indistinguishable from mid-20th century US liberals. From this standpoint, folks like West and Sanders can safely deliver vague socialist talking points while serving as social democrats, but are ultimately limited by their peculiar faith in US democracy and reformism, which becomes even more problematic by their anti-communism.

West's constant yearning for unity among the people, while certainly commendable and needed, can and has led to extending an open hand to elements of the working class who are likely irredeemable, if not simply dangerous, due to their fierce bigotry, intense xenophobia, and blatant misogyny. And his unwillingness to commit to forceful politics over vague intellectualism has led him to make problematic assessments, one of which included a tweet from 2011, in which he oddly proclaimed Ronald Reagan as "a freedom fighter in terms of supporting our Jewish bros [and] sis in the Soviet Union [and] opposing vicious forms of communism."[11]

Granted, this tweet was made as part of a series of tweets that addressed Barack Obama's public adoration of Reagan—ironically stating, "this glorification of Ronald Reagan is really a sad commentary on our lack of historical consciousness,"[12] and concluding that Obama was

---

11   Cornel West (@CornelWest), "Ronald Reagan was a freedom fighter in terms of supporting our Jewish bros & sis in the Soviet Union & opposing vicious forms of communism," Twitter, Jan. 8, 2011, 1:10 p.m., twitter.com/CornelWest/status/23848928873021440?lang=en.

12   Cornel West (@CornelWest), "But this glorification of Ronald Reagan is

"chasing the cheap fantasy of bipartisanship." But, nonetheless, it provides a good example on how the weight of anti-communism, which seems to be holding West hostage, can be a potentially blinding force during a time when it, as a direct product of Nazism and fascism, needs to be snuffed out once and for all. In the end, such a blind spot is not only a massive liability, but also seemingly suggests the potential to drift back into the hands of the Democratic Party.

Can Any Significant Change Come From Participating in Bourgeois Elections?

Oddly enough, if any significant change comes from this campaign, it will exist outside the realm of electoral politics. We would be foolish to believe that 1) West can win, and 2) even if he did win, he would have the power to single-handedly enact policies that would benefit the working class. While this may sound defeatist, it is not. The reality is that the US government and its entire political system are not only completely controlled by the will of capital, but were deliberately set up by its founders for this very reason: "to protect the opulent minority from the toiling majority,"[13] to paraphrase James Madison.

Does this mean the working class has never won meaningful concessions from the government, via electoral politics? Of course not. Bourgeois democracy, despite its deliberate orientation as a force of capital, has represented a battleground between the class interests of the capitalist minority and the working-class majority in the past. In fact, during times of capitalist crises, the system has responded in ways that have resulted in very real concessions for the working class. In the US, the most notable period that included such concessions came during the 1930s, when "New Deal" policies were implemented in response to the Great Depression. Throughout the 20th century, Keynesianism represented the primary macroeconomic policy direction deployed by the

---

really a sad commentary on our lack of historical consciousness," Twitter, Jan. 8, 2011, 1:15 p.m., x.com/CornelWest/status/23850186212122624.

13   James Madison in Farrand, *Records*, I, 430–31, ctd. in *Term of the Senate*, June 26, 1787, accessed online at: https://founders.archives.gov/documents/Madison/01-10-02-0044.

government in its management of capital, using high tax rates on corporations and the wealthy to fund governmental programs designed to both supplement capitalist growth and soften the systemic parasitism of that growth. And, in the 1960s, coming on the heels of radical uprisings throughout the country—most notably, the antiwar and Civil Rights movements—"Great Society" policies were created to provide more assistance and opportunities to working people.

It should be noted, though, that the underlying reasons for many of these concessions were tactical, as they have been made to prevent a radical or revolutionary break from the dominant capitalist/imperialist system. In other words, they were just as much forms of appeasement issued by the capitalist class, for the sake of their own survival, as they were hard-fought gains won by the working class, for our betterment. Many gains were the direct result of organized labor struggles, but were also made possible by the US military's brutalization and looting campaigns of the Global South via colonialism and imperialism. They were also products of the US's advantageous post-world-war-two positioning, the Marshall Plan, and the fact that US infrastructure was virtually untouched by the ravages of the war. And much of these gains excluded black and brown members of the US working class, as well as women, all of whom continued to be relegated to hyper-exploited positions within the working class, often confined to internal colonies and subjected to compounded social and material forms of oppression. These inconsistencies, as well as the inability of these reforms to affect the modes of production, left such legislation vulnerable to both circumvention and rollbacks.

It is important to include context behind these concessions because we must understand, first and foremost, that all of capitalist society rests upon a fundamental class struggle between those who own and control the means of production (capitalists) and those of us whose only chance for survival is to sell our labor to those owners (workers). With this understanding, we can see that societal progression, or regression, is the result of this dialectical battle. The sobering reality for the working class is that capitalists always have the upper hand because they have claimed ownership of the means we use to function and survive. And, while capitalist governments like that of the United States have awarded us some rights, and have occasionally given us some concessions, they are ultimately tools that are wielded by the capitalist class to maintain their dominance over us.

Thus, bourgeois (capitalist) democracy is a brilliant scheme for the (capitalist) ruling class because it gives off the appearance of freedom via constitutional documents, legal systems, voting, and a variety of supposed civil/human rights. Beneath the facade are extremely strict power dynamics represented primarily by these class distinctions (again, the minority class who own/control property and the means of production overseeing the majority class whose only basis of survival is our labor). The working-class masses are repressed and controlled in nearly every way possible within this arrangement. Injustice is a daily part of our lives that we learn to accept to survive the drudgery.

In some instances, where gross injustices occur, we are awarded the "right" to appeal to the systems that exist on the surface, but this "right" always places the burden of proof on us. Therefore, since we have no time, money, energy, and resources to dedicate to these processes (because we're all working our lives away while living paycheck to paycheck), it is incredibly rare for any sort of justice to materialize against a powerful state/class that has seemingly unlimited amounts of time, money, energy, and resources to oppose us. In this never-ending, losing scenario, the ruling class and all of their institutions (including schools and media) can simply say: "we gave you inalienable rights and encourage you to use them if you feel wronged," knowing very well these rights, and the systems put in place to exercise them, are nothing but manufactured dead ends hidden behind virtual freeways.

This systemic understanding brings us back to the question at hand: can significant change come from bourgeois elections? If we were to look at the history of the US, we would surely conclude that it can, as noted above. However, when looking at capitalism as the regressive system that it *now* is—due to its fascistic foundation of claiming "private property" as a social relationship for capital to employ (exploit) labor; its birth from trillions of dollars of "free capital" generated by chattel slavery; its tendency to centralize wealth and, thus, political/social/governmental power; its cancer-like need for never-ending growth; its bloodlust for expansion and theft via war; and its array of elements that are riddled with internal contradictions which only worsen over time due to perpetually falling rates of profit—we should understand that it has reached a very late stage. In other words, the concessions that were made in the past are, quite frankly, no longer possible. The formation of an industrialized—albeit, mostly white—"middle class" was an anomaly only made possible by the unique stages of historical development that existed in the 20th century.

The capitalist coup called "neoliberalism" put an end to all of that.[14] And it did so during a period of time (1970s/80s) when falling rates of profit were decimating the Keynesian model, the gold standard was removed, monopoly capitalism became entrenched, corporate governance (what Mussolini himself referred to as "fascism") was cemented, and globalization and financialization became prominent factors in wealth extraction. Pro-capitalists will claim all of these things are "artificial mutations" of "true, free-market" capitalism, caused by "too much government involvement," but the truth is they are mature stages of capitalism that were inevitable, absent a socialist revolution. Clever terms like "cronyism" and "corporatism" merely refer to *natural developments* caused by capital accumulation (and, conversely, widespread dispossession) and the concentration of wealth and power that has allowed capitalists to gain control of all aspects of society, including the entirety of government.

The sobering lesson from all of this is that any meaningful concessions from the capitalist class (via the electoral arena) will likely never materialize during capitalism's late stages. The system has become so cannibalistic and riddled with crises that it has been feeding on itself for at least the past forty years. The industrialized "middle class," or aristocracy of labor, has been all but destroyed, small capitalists are being devoured by big capitalists, and the economic system has become fully intertwined with the government. Thus, we are already decades deep into a very real transition from covert fascism to overt fascism, as the system scrambles to shield itself from crises after crises.

---

14   See Colin Jenkins, "The Capitalist Coup Called Neoliberalism: How and Why it Went Down," *Hampton Institute*, 27 June 2019. Available online at: https://www.hamptonthink.org/read/the-capitalist-coup-called-neoliberalism-how-and-why-it-went-down.

During this process, capitalism has been propped up by so many tricks and tactics coming from the capitalist state—corporate subsidies, quantitative easing ("printing money"), constant meddling by the federal reserve, etc.—that it is too far gone to respond to the needs of the people. These tricks and tactics are *necessary* for the system's survival; or, in more precise terms, necessary to protect and maintain the wealth of the capitalist minority, by further degrading the working-class majority and perpetually "kicking the can down the road." But, this road comes to an end. And we are fast approaching that end.

The only thing that capitalists and their state are concerned with now is protecting themselves from the imminent collapse, which means we're already well into a significant fascist transition. The fact that unfathomable amounts of money are being thrown at the military and police during a time when tent cities, homelessness, and drug overdoses are taking over every major city, and working people everywhere cannot afford rent or food, tells us that the US government, which is a direct manifestation of the capitalist class, is unable to see past its own interests to avert this collapse. So, it has chosen to dig in and protect the increasingly wealthy minority from the increasingly desperate majority.

West will not have a chance to win the election, and will likely not even capture a miniscule percentage of the vote. He may not even make the ballots in most states. And, even worse yet, if he were to win the election in some dream scenario and assume "the highest office in the land," nothing substantial would come from it. Because the system was set up to represent wealth (or capital), not people. And the days of meaningful capitalist concessions are long gone.

Despite this, West and his campaign should approach the election with the intent to win, because that is the way to build genuine momentum. But, in this process, the focus must be on building a new world from the ravages of the inevitable collapse. This is where our time, energy, and resources should be, and should have been for decades now, but we've been too enamored with bourgeois politics to begin that transition. However, it's not too late to regroup and refocus. And West's campaign, like Bernie's campaigns, can be a catalyst for this shift. Bernie sold out, chose his career, and failed. West might succeed in serving as a launching pad—if he chooses the correct path.

Should Working-Class People Support Cornel West's Campaign?

We need to divest from bourgeois politics and the capitalist system. A campaign like West's, which will ironically occur within the bourgeois electoral arena, could be a major catalyst for such a divestment. So, what do we need to understand, and what will West—or any truly progressive candidate—need to do, to stay on the right path?

1. We need to understand that electoral politics are both a time sink and a dead end *if* the goal is to win elections, assume office, and enact legislation. Therefore, campaigns should only be used to educate, agitate, and form counter-hegemonic and liberatory institutions and organizations.

2. We need to understand that building working-class consciousness is the primary need at this moment in time. Challenging capitalist propaganda from mainstream media, providing knowledge and historical context, and offering reality-based narratives as a counter to the extreme paranoia and delusion pushed by capitalist media is the way to do this.

3. We need to understand that authentic working-class (that is, a left-wing) politics must be built from the ground up in the United States. It must initially be anti-capitalist, anti-imperialist, and rooted in the working-class struggle against the capitalist ruling class. In this process, any remnants of anti-communism, which are almost always products of fear and/or ignorance, must be ironed out.

4. We need to understand that liberal identity politics and culture wars are being disseminated by the ruling class to whip up hysteria among the masses, cause widespread confusion and misdirected rage, and keep the working class not only further divided, but constantly at each other's throats. We must challenge this head-on by keeping the focus on class struggle while, at the same time, not allowing for bigoted elements to fester, as they are mere remnants of capitalist culture and naturally anti-working-class.

5. We need to understand that fascism is already here in the US, and it has always been here for many of the hyper-marginalized members of the working class. This understanding includes the

knowledge that the capitalist system has become fully intertwined with the capitalist government and is being protected by both capitalist political parties. In other words, Democrats are *not* anti-fascist; they are just as much a part of the transition to overt fascism as Republicans are.

6. We need to understand that formidable working-class institutions and organizations need to be built *now*, because time is running out. These organizations and institutions must exist completely outside the realm of electoral politics, which means they must be organized, funded, and maintained by us, with no ties to, or relationships with, bourgeois politicians, the capitalist parties, or the US government.

What will West and his campaign need to do to make this happen?

1. West and his campaign must understand that the purpose of this run is not to win, assume office, and enact legislation. It is also not to build a political party to do these things moving forward. If those things happen to occur as a corollary development, then fine, but the primary goal should be to use this platform to radicalize (that is, educate) and organize the US working class.

2. West and his campaign must use this platform to promote working-class consciousness. This can be done by attacking mainstream (capitalist) narratives head-on, offering counter-narratives based in reality, and deconstructing the hysteria and paranoia being disseminated by the media.

3. West and his campaign must show what a true left looks like. This means that he must be unapologetically radical by exposing the roots of our problems, which are not things like immigration, inflation, and "corruption," but rather are capitalist modes and arrangements of production, imperialism, and the bourgeois state, which has been intentionally constructed to shield these roots. He should expect red-baiting and take ownership of it without fear of being "unelectable," which is easy to do if you are not ultimately concerned with winning an election. He should be openly socialist. He should be clear about what socialism actually is—the people owning and controlling the means that are used to sustain society.

He should be clear that the welfare state is not socialism, but rather a necessity of capitalism. He should be clear that social democracy is merely a softer version of capitalism that simply cannot be maintained because of the predatory nature of the capitalist class in this late stage. Using very clear wording, even technical wording, goes against West's oratorical style, but he must make an effort to include such deliberate terminology along with his traditionally soulful approach.

4. West and his campaign need to keep the focus on class struggle by avoiding the inevitable pitfalls of liberal identity politics and culture wars. This does not mean ignoring the social realities of marginalized identities, which of course are naturally intertwined with class oppression, but rather by constantly keeping the focus on the basis of class. This is something West has done exceptionally well in the past and there is no reason why this should not continue moving forward on this particular stage.

5. West and his campaign need to express the reality that fascism is already here in the United States and is in a transitional period from being covert (in that it has always existed in the margins as well as in the foundation of both capitalism and the United States) to overt. He must explain that fascism is capitalism in decay. He must explain that the exponential funding of the military and police by the capitalist class and its government will naturally come home to roost on the entirety of the US working class. And he must publicly rid himself of the belief that Democrats are allies in the fight against fascism.

6. West and his campaign must use this platform to build actual organizations and institutions, on the ground, throughout the country, funded and maintained by the people. These organizations and institutions must be constructed to last far beyond this campaign and must be built with the understanding that they will never work with bourgeois institutions, including the government and political parties owned by the capitalist class. These organizations should exist to meet the most basic needs of the people: food programs, clinics, self-defense, political education, ideological development, etc. all rooted in a working-class culture formed in direct

contrast to bourgeois culture.

A Means to an End?

From a dialectical perspective, Cornel West's presidential bid is a seemingly positive development for the working-class masses in our struggle against the forces of capital. This is not necessarily saying much, as we have had very little reason to pay attention to, let alone participate in, bourgeois elections for quite some time. Thus, this is not positive because West has any chance of winning or assuming office—he does not—but because it provides us the opportunity to finally break away from the stranglehold of bourgeois politics and the two capitalist/imperialist political parties. We should seek to use this campaign as a way to build our own proletariat infrastructure throughout the country—community centers, clinics, food programs, networks, schools, etc.—something that will be needed as both the capitalist system and the US government continue their rapid descent into overt fascism.

As West throws down the gauntlet against what he and many others see as systemic ills, he will find himself stuck between two vastly different worlds: one where the masses of people desperately need, and I believe are ready for, an unapologetically radical candidate from the left; and another where dominant society and its very real mechanisms of capitalist violence and oppression will simply not allow this need to be delivered. The best thing West can do at this moment is dedicate himself to serving this need. Whether or not he and his campaign choose to use this opportunity as such a catalyst remains to be seen.

By all signs, Cornel West is a social democrat. And, history tells us we should be very wary of the compromising nature of social democrats. So, we should be skeptical. We should continue working on our own efforts and projects to construct authentic, working-class organizations and institutions. We should pace ourselves and not throw too much energy, physical or emotional, behind West and his campaign. But we should also give this a chance to serve our needs—use it as a potential tool whose frequency can increase if we find it on the right path, or decrease and even be discarded if it becomes clear that it will not be fruitful. We should attempt to steer it in the right direction because it is the best option we have been given on this type of platform, if only for the fact that it exists outside the Democratic Party.

Our present reality is dismal. Our immediate future is dystopian. Capitalism is rotting away and taking us with it. Fascism is here. The capitalist government and all of its institutions are clearly responding by choosing an increasingly predatory and barbaric direction. We must forge our own way, dig ourselves in, and prepare for the absolute worst while building our own institutions that show the promise of a better world.

SECTION 4
The Struggle Over Subjectivity

CHAPTER 10
PRIDE MEANS FIGHT BACK: NOTES ON THE PERSISTENCE OF LGBTQ OPPRESSION

Alla Ivanchikova

ALLA IVANCHIKOVA is an associate professor of English and Comparative Literature at Hobart and William Smith Colleges in upstate New York. She is the author of *Imagining Afghanistan: Global Fiction and Film of the 9/11 Wars* (Purdue University Press, 2019) and co-editor of *The Future of Lenin: Power, Politics, and Revolution in the Twenty-First Century* (Albany: SUNY, 2022). Her articles have appeared in *Modern Fiction Studies*, *Textual Practice*, *Camera Obscura*, and *College Literature*, among many others. She is currently working on a new monograph, tentatively titled *Technoimmortality: An Unfinished Project*.

"PRIDE MEANS FIGHT BACK" was the slogan we picked when pride became political again in the summer of 2023. Trans and queer people's rights were under attack everywhere. I and a small group of organizers from upstate New York traveled to every Pride in the region that would have us talk to people about what they were going through and if they wanted to organize together. I was surprised by the number of refugees we met from other states—places that have become increasingly hostile to their LGBTQ residents. Some told us stories about how they decided to move to New York, still a state where LGBTQ rights are protected, for the sake of their children, their families, mental health, safety, access to medical care, and so on. I talked for a while to such refugees from Florida, Ohio, and Arkansas. Florida has recently targeted its LGBTQ population with a slew of new laws, from the infamous "Don't Say Gay" law to a bill that banned gender-affirming care, and a resonant anti-drag bill that threatens to take the culture to a pre-Stonewall era. Arkansas was the first state to ban gender-affirming treatments to minors in 2021, in a vote overturning the veto of a Republican Governor, Asa Hutchinson who thought the bill was "too extreme" and targeted an already "vulnerable population."[1] After a decade during which trans and queer people in the US felt relatively optimistic about their prospects of integration into the social fabric, the specter of oppression was looming large again: there was fear for personal safety, anger, despair, and people on the move, crossing state lines. When people decide to leave everything behind and uproot themselves, it's serious business: no one makes such a decision lightly. Many expressed profound disappointment: why is this happening again? Why isn't the progress we had fought for more lasting? Can we hope for the end of oppression?

As an activist-scholar with Marxist roots, I knew these were in fact not easy questions. Can we hope for the end of LGBTQ oppression under capitalism? The subject of the enduring basis of LGBTQ oppression has preoccupied theorists for quite some time and was the issue hotly debated by Marxist, poststructuralist, feminist, and psychoanalytically-minded academics throughout the 1980-90s. Some thinkers on the left argued, during that era, that there is no class basis for LBGTQ oppression, and that the fight for LGBTQ rights was about the politics of recognition (was thus merely cultural, concerning changes in the superstructure). It was argued that while sexist or racial division results in empirically observable economic exploitation of the oppressed group, LGBTQ people do not constitute an economically oppressed category in the same way as these other groups. Nancy Fraser wrote, famously, in 1995:

Sexuality [...] is a mode of social differentiation whose roots do not lie in the political economy, as homosexuals are distributed throughout the entire class structure of capitalist society, occupy no distinctive position in the division of labour, and do not constitute an exploited class. Rather, their mode of collectivity is that of a despised sexuality, rooted in the cultural-valuational structure of society. From this perspective, the

---

1 Vanessa Romo, "Arkansas Gov. Asa Hutchinson On Transgender Health Care Bill: 'Step Way Too Far,'" *NPR* April 6, 2021. Available here: https://www.npr.org/2021/04/06/984884294/arkansas-gov-asa-hutchinson-on-transgender-health-care-bill-step-way-too-far

injustice they suffer is quintessentially a matter of recognition.[2]

It's easy to understand why such a claim was made. Racial capitalism—a term introduced by Cedric Robinson—is a horrific system of value extraction from entire populations.[3] Unwaged labor done by women is a source of surplus value for the capitalist class. There are of course economic losses trans/queer people suffer; for instance, trans and queer youth are more likely to end up homeless; and trans women, and especially trans women of color, often lose access to wage employment and end up outside mainstream wage economy. Yet, one doesn't speak of "wages of heterosexuality" (or "cisgender wages") in the same way as some speak about the accumulated "wages of whiteness;" there is no particular type of work, such as reproductive work, that LGBTQ people do, and for which they can demand wages, similar to how the International Wages for Housework Committee demanded wages due to women for unpaid work.[4] Unfortunately, Marx and Engels did not leave us a developed theory of sexuality and gender expression. Marxist (and Marxism-adjacent) thinkers have proposed many perspectives from which to consider the basis and the persistence of LGBTQ oppression throughout history and into the capitalist era; there are three lines of argumentation that are most common:

1. LGBTQ oppression plays a key role in fortifying the sexual division of labor;

2. LGBTQ oppression protects the existing system of social re-

---

2 See Nancy Frazer, "From Redistribution to Recognition? Dilemmas of Justice in a 'Post-Socialist' Age," where she distinguishes between socioeconomic injustice and cultural injustice. *New Left Review* 1.212 (1995). "The remedy for cultural injustice," she argues, is not economic redistribution, but "some sort of cultural or symbolic change." Available here: https://newleftreview.org/issues/i212/articles/nancy-fraser-from-redistribution-to-recognition-dilemmas-of-justice-in-a-post-socialist-age

3 Cedric Robinson, *Black Marxism: The making of the black radical tradition* (Chapel Hill: University of North Carolina Press, 1983).

4 W.E.B. Du Bois spoke of whiteness as a form of wage in his *Black Reconstruction in America* (New Brunswick: Transaction Publishers, 1935). On the history of Wages for Work campaign, see article by Louise Toupin, "The History of Wages of Housework." Available here: https://www.plutobooks.com/blog/wages-housework-campaign-history/

production;

3. LGBTQ oppression is used as an instrument of class struggle to divide the working class.

It is likely that all these factors contribute to the persistence of LGBTQ oppression we see today in the US and beyond. Contrary to Fraser's claim, these factors concern not just cultural norms (the politics of recognition), but the socioeconomic basis, suggesting that to eliminate LGBTQ oppression we'd have to change not just the culture, but the way society is organized. Let me briefly discuss these three lines of explanation.

LGBTQ Oppression and the Sexual Division of Labor

US Marxist philosopher Fredric Jameson suggests that phenomena such as women's oppression are not in themselves caused by capitalism but are residual—a leftover from prior social formations.[5] Sexual and gender repression was not brought by capitalism; in fact, they predate capitalism by millennia. Engels speculated that the oppression of women had its origins, most likely, in the early hierarchical societies that emerged with the transition from nomadic hunter-gatherer lifestyles to the agricultural mode of production. In *The Origins of the Family, Private Property, and the State,* he provides an account of this transition, arguing that private property, the monogamous family, and patriarchy emerge at the same time and are interrelated. For the first time in their history, humans gain access to a surplus of food that some can then begin to accumulate. Engels famously talked of "the world historical defeat of women" that took place during this transition: the accumulation of surplus wealth created the conditions for the idea of private property to develop—property that could be inherited (and now passed from father to son). Monogamy became important so that fathers could trace their offspring. Men became property owners and women ended up on the side of property. The system that emerged was based on what anthropologists call "the exchange of women": women "circulate," either as a

---

5   See Jameson, *The Political Unconscious* (Ithaca: Cornell University Press, 1982). The terms "residual," "dominant," and "emergent" were introduced into Marxist cultural analysis by Raymond Williams; see his *Marxism and Literature* (Oxford: Oxford University Press, 1978).

means of forming kinship ties between households or clans or as a form of payment or debt settlement. The "residue" of the practice of the exchange of women is still evident today in the custom of a father giving away his daughter in marriage.

Engels's views have been fiercely debated for more than a century. While some of the anthropological work Engels relies on has been disputed, the central insights of the work still stand. Notably, where, say, Sigmund Freud viewed women's inferiority as biological (anatomy is destiny), insisting as late as in 1938 on the centrality of penis envy in the psychological life of a woman, Engels viewed women's oppression as an utterly contingent historical phenomenon—a patriarchal coup—in which one group (men) had made itself dominant over another group (women) and in such a way that a class division had been established. He writes: "The first class opposition that appears in history coincides with the development of the antagonism between man and woman in monogamous marriage, and the first class oppression coincides with that of the female sex by the male."[6] In a non-monogamous group marriage, such an opposition does not exist. Patriarchy, for Engels, emerges as a result of the overthrow of what he, following anthropologist Johann J. Bahofen, calls the "Mother-right" (classless, collectivist, matrilineal societies where group marriage rather than monogamous marriage was the norm) and marks the advent of the new, class-based world in which "prosperity and development for some is won through the misery and frustration of others." Engels' central insight is this: because patriarchy is a contingent form that has a historical origin, it can and will be undone by the forces of human history. While Engels didn't write on the question of homosexuality and doesn't speak of heteropatriarchy, his basic insights can be put into productive dialogue with more recent, more nuanced theories of sexuality and gender. During the gay liberation era, queer theorist Gayle Rubin pointed out, in her work "The Traffic in Women: Notes on the Political Economy of Sex" (1975), that the prohibition of homosexuality is central to the exchange of women, and in obvious ways—something that Engels himself failed to notice but which follows from his argument. The exchange of women can only

---

6   Friedrich Engels."Origins of the Family, Private Property, and the State, "The Family: The Monogamous Family," accessed online at: https://www.marxists.org/archive/marx/works/1884/origin-family/ch02d.htm.

work in a binary system of gender that is strictly enforced, where homosexuality or gender non-conformity is prohibited. Gender rebellion, she argues, would throw a wrench into the machinery of the system where women are treated as currency circulating, among other things, as debt payments between clans. Rubin writes: "What would happen if our hypothetical woman not only refused the man to whom she was promised, but asked for a woman instead? If a single refusal were disruptive, a double refusal would be insurrectionary. [...] If two women managed to extricate themselves from the debt nexus, two other women would have to be found to replace them."[7] The regulation of what we today would refer to as minoritized sexualities and gender identities, is, for Rubin, necessary for the functioning of kinship systems based on the principle of male dominance. Patriarchy emerges as heteropatriarchy. The two types of oppression are interrelated; both emerge long before capitalism and go hand-in-hand, surviving into our era as a residual phenomenon, but repurposed and redeployed, as we'll see below, in capitalism.

Importantly, Engels connects patriarchy with the emergence of a particular form of property: private property over land, cattle, and tools. And conversely, he envisions that the abolition of private property of the means of production will bring a monumental change in the structure of human kinship: monogamous (patriarchal) family will fade away as its material basis disappears. Other forms of relationality and kinship will emerge; a profound restructuring of gender relations and sexuality will take place. In an earlier work, "The Principles of Communism" (1847), Engels describes this vision: a transition to communism "will transform the relations between the sexes into a purely private matter which concerns only the persons involved and into which society has no occasion to intervene. It can do this since it does away with private property and educates children on a communal basis, and in this way removes the two bases of traditional marriage—the dependence rooted in private property, of the woman on the man, and of the children on the parents."[8] This line of argumentation becomes important to

---

7   Gayle Rubin, "The Traffic in Women," in *Toward an Anthropology of Women*, ed. Rayna R. Reyter (New York: Monthly Review Press, 1975), 183.

8   See section titled "What will be the influence of communist society on the family?" Available here: https://www.marxists.org/archive/marx/works/1847/11/prin-com.htm

21st-century trans communists who are family abolitionists. They point out that early 20th-century socialists made attempts at building sexually liberated societies and took modest steps towards abolishing the nuclear family. Alexandra Kollontai, a Bolshevik revolutionary and later Soviet ambassador whom Sophie Lewis calls "a glamorous high femme libertine and family abolitionist" formulated "a glass of water" theory—a belief that sexuality will be transformed away from scarcity of the couple form and towards the plenitude of communist love in a communist society.[9] Today, trans/queer communist theorists sketch a horizon of family abolitionism to forge an image of a world liberated from residual forms of oppression. They insist that we must think beyond the family if we want to imagine the fulfillment of the promise of trans/queer liberation after the revolution abolishes economic suffering and need. It is the communist commune, and not the family, that is the caregiving unit where queer and trans peoples' identities can flourish, argues M.E. O'Brien. She writes: "In the communization of society and the abolition of the family, [...] gender could become what is already prefigured in trans experience: gender as a form of expressing subtle personal truth, the beauty and richness of human expression, and the wielding of aesthetics towards personal fulfillment."[10] The nuclear family is a residual form that, ultimately, would not serve us well: a child, especially a trans/queer/nonbinary child, would need access to a wider range of mentors, role models, and people who manifest a variety of gender identities and forms of self. A larger commune, O'Brien underscores, would serve as a check against the arbitrary prejudice that children (especially trans and queer children and youth) so often experience in biological families.

Family and Social Reproduction

The second line of argumentation states that capitalism relies on the hetero-patriarchal family for the work of social reproduction. Capitalism, it is maintained, redeploys the sex/gender system[11] it inherits in contradictory ways. Consider this: early industrial capitalism was a frontal assault

---

9   Sophie Lewis, *Abolish the Family* (Brooklyn: Verso, 2022), 53.

10   M.E. O'Brien, *Family Abolition: Capitalism and the Communizing of Care* (London: Pluto Press, 2023), 232.

11   Rubin's term.

on the patriarchal family structure of the peasant. When peasants, driven off the land, flocked to urban centers in search of work, traditional family structures and relations were destined to buckle and melt into thin air. As Engels observed in *The Conditions of the Working Class in England* (1845), workers' deplorable living conditions effectively destroyed families. Workers often shared rooms with dozens of other laborers—women, men, children hunkering together, with no expectation of privacy or nuclear family boundaries. Women and children worked long hours and were often ruthlessly exploited; there were no boundaries or guardrails protecting the "sanctity" of childhood: these emerged out of the workers' struggle later. It is observing this, no doubt, that made Engels conclude that capitalism is eroding the very foundations of patriarchy and the nuclear family, paving the way for socialist gender equality and sexual freedom. Historically, mass migration of landless peasants to cities also created the conditions for the emergence of subcultures in which people with minoritized genders and sexualities found each other, came to consciousness of themselves as a group, and began their struggle for liberation. As LGBTQ historian John D'Emilio points out, wage labor created conditions for corporeal and sexual autonomy; insofar as these individuals no longer had to rely on their communities of origin for survival, they were also freed from these communities' norms.[12] Sarah Waters's novels such as *Fingersmith* or *Tipping the Velvet* bring to life the emerging sexual subcultures of Victorian-era London. As industrial capitalism began to create conditions for LGBTQ liberation, however, 19th century medical science began pathologizing homosexuality and the law criminalized it. As Christopher Chitty shows, in his study *Sexual Hegemony,* the bourgeoisie used sexual repression (specifically, the policing of male homosexuality) both to discipline the working poor and to harass the aristocracy—its rival class.[13]

So, does capitalism really need heteropatriarchy? On the one hand, it doesn't seem so: the sexual orientation and gender expression of the worker are of no importance to the capitalist class insofar as surplus value can be extracted from their labor. That's why Silicon Valley cor-

---

[12] John D'Emilio, "Capitalism and Gay Identity," in *Making Trouble: Essays on Gay History, Politics, and the University* (New York: Routledge, 1992).

[13] Christopher Chitty, *Statecraft, Sodomy, and Capital in the Rise of the World System* (Durham: Duke University Press, 2020).

porations adopt non-discrimination policies as they compete for talent globally. It *does* "get better"[14] in some pockets of the capitalist world. However, if that were true, what would account for the persistence of sexual and gender oppression throughout the twentieth century and into the current times, and its unfortunate return after periods of "liberation"? Some argue that LGBTQ oppression is important to capitalism because of the way capitalism structures social reproduction and that this imposes limits on how far liberation can go. According to this argument, capitalism needs the family as a site of privatized reproduction where the next generation of workers is produced and where surplus value is generated via the unpaid labor of caring for the family (traditionally, women's work). Working (and middle) class women are slotted for the double-shift: waged labor outside of the home and unwaged reproductive labor at home. To do this, women must be disciplined and seduced into the social value system where this work is seen as "the labor of love" and is done freely for the sake of the children; they must be taught to view marriage as a reward, a badge of honor, an achievement, rather than a bait-and-switch scheme that traps them into decades of unpaid work. Gender outlaws, such as LGBTQ folks, challenge this gendered arrangement by virtue of their insubordination.

In the 1990s, philosopher Judith Butler argued that heterosexuality is a fragile system that only works by constantly reproducing itself via repetition.[15] It's like a meme that has gone viral: when people stop sharing it, it dies. She argued that just like with other replicators, there is nothing natural about it; like a gene, like a meme, like fashion, it only seems natural while it's dominant (widely cited). That's why when trans/queer people stop "citing" the normative code of heterosexuality, modify it, parody it, or begin speaking a different code altogether, they are seen as dangerous because they put the whole system at risk. Butler's analysis, even though conveyed in obscure academic lingo, resonated with many people and she became one of the most quoted theorists in the world. (Butler is still singled out by the far-right as the foundational

---

14 This is a reference to "It Gets Better" campaign to which many members of US corporate cultures contributed. Available here: https://itgetsbetter.org/videos/

15 See, for instance, Judith Butler, "Imitation and Gender Insubordination" in The Critical Tradition, Third Edition, edited by David H. Richter (New York: Bedford/St.Martin, 2007), 1707-1718.

figure for what they call "gender ideology.") To apply this to the question of social reproduction, trans/queer folks are a rogue element that throws a wrench into the machinery of heteronormative social reproduction that relies on the majority of people accepting the norm: a nuclear family—mom and dad—with two or three children in tow.

At the height of the gay liberation era, LGBTQ communities attempted to create alternative institutions of social reproduction. Having found themselves excised from the hetero-reproductive family culture, LGBTQ communities, by the 1960s, began to systematically create alternative kinship systems in opposition to the heteropatriarchal household. Separatist lesbian communes, families of choice, queer "houses," and collectively run households emerged in the 1970s in an effort to reimagine social reproduction.[16] In the midst of the AIDS crisis, LGBTQ groups organized communal systems of care delivery. Moreover, since the 1970s, LGBTQ writers, theorists, and activists conjured imaginaries of the world not organized around the primacy of heteropatriarchal reproduction. LGBTQ theorists exposed the heteropatriarchal family structure as the site of replication of capitalist values.[17] Jack Halberstam writes of the rhythms of "reproductive time" as early to bed, early to rise; separation of work and play; separation of private and public, as key to disciplining workers in capitalism: controlled by the high reproductive workload and instant indebtedness that comes with having children in a capitalist society, parents in heteropatriarchal families turn compliant and docile, politically inactive, inclined to avoid upheaval and change for the sake of their children.[18] In sum, while struggling for equal rights, the LGBTQ movement, during the gay/queer liberation era, also sought to redefine family and imagine a world beyond privatized reproduction.

During the AIDS crisis, however, when the LGBTQ community

---

16 Netflix show *Pose* is centered around the culture of "Houses"—a phenomenon that made people curious about the cultures of trans/queer social reproduction. See, for instance, an article by Elena Nicolaou, "Already Obsessed With Pose? Here's A History Of New York's Ball Culture," June 4, 2018, *Refinery29*. Available here: https://www.refinery29.com/en-us/2018/06/200854/ball-culture-history-pose-fx .

17 See, for instance, Michael Warner, *The Trouble with Normal: Sex, Politics, and the Ethics of Queer Life* (Cambridge: Harvard University Press, 1999).

18 See Halberstam, *In a Queer Time and Place: Transgender Bodies, Subcultural Lives* (New York: New York University Press, 2005).

had to reorient from utopian thinking to surviving the catastrophe, the Reagan administration weaponized the rhetoric of American "family values" and assumed a sinister anti-LGBTQ stance in order to reconsolidate the family as a site of care provision.[19] This, sociologist Melinda Cooper explains, was part of the transition from Keynesian welfare capitalism to the neoliberal model of the 1980s where the nuclear family began to serve as a kind of "mutual insurance contract" designed to replace the "'impersonal' bonds of social insurance." Targeting gay people in the name of the "family" was a cover for the removal of social wealth for the majority of American workers. Cooper writes, "Cuts to public funding in healthcare, education, and welfare have pushed people back toward kinship-based forms of self-care and mutual support and the expansion of consumer credit has turned household deficit-spending into a substitute for state deficit-spending."[20] Cooper's study clearly shows that anti-LGBTQ rhetoric and the rhetoric of hetero-reproductive family values did not benefit heterosexual families: it meant a loss of real earning power for everyone.

So, does capitalism *really* need heteropatriarchy? Yes and no: capitalism in itself does not care about family or the heavily mythologized family values any more than it cares about the sexual preferences or gender identities of the workers. Philosopher Michel Foucault (a foundational figure for LGBTQ studies) showed the futility of the "repression hypothesis": capitalism does not need to repress sexuality. Occasionally, it could be as much in the interests of capital to allow sexual identities to proliferate, to encourage consumption based on these varied preferences. And yet, we see that the capitalist class continues to periodically weaponize (heterosexual, reproductive) family values, for which LGBTQ people serve as a foil, especially when it needs the family to carry the burden of social reproduction—giving birth to and raising children; caring for the elderly; cooking, cleaning, and maintaining one's dwelling;

---

19   See the wonderful documentary *United in Anger: A History of Act Up*, which documents the community's struggle of the AIDS years, as well as the Act Up Oral History Project, both spearheaded by the activist and writer Sarah Schulman (https://actuporalhistory.org/). The documentary is available here: https://www.unitedinanger.com/.

20   "Family Matters," *Viewpoint Magazine* Mar. 19, 2018. Available here: https://viewpointmag.com/2018/03/19/family-matters/

providing emotional and care work; and caring for the millions disabled by the pandemic. So, until the bulk of social reproduction is collectivized (considered to be a responsibility of all) and systems for such care are established, there will be a material basis for such periodic return of "family values" even after periods of LGBTQ "liberation."

Anti-LGBTQ Populist Rhetoric Dividing the Working Class

In the summer of 2023, a city councilor in the small town in upstate New York where I live made hateful anti-LGBTQ comments (making an association between LGBTQ people and pedophilia) on his social media, and a portion of the town rebelled. Queers, trans people, and allies made placards and flocked to the city council meeting to express their anger and frustration, demanding the councilor's censure. In an economically depressed town where working-class people should have been upset about inflation, rising food and gas prices, and high unemployment, they were instead divided by social media posts about LGBTQ people made by someone in power. The hate the councilor sputtered didn't exist in a vacuum but in a national and global context where LGBTQ lives were put increasingly in danger in the service of political aims. In recent years, Brazil's former president Jair Bolsonaro, openly homophobic, used anti-LGBTQ rhetoric to foment division within the largely Catholic working class, further endangering the lives of trans/queer people in a country with a high LGBTQ murder rate. In Hungary, ultra-right head of state Victor Orban earned global notoriety by declaring war on what he called "gender ideology." His first highstakes target in this war was Central European University (CEU), home to one of the very few Gender Studies programs in the region. Orban declared Gender Studies unscientific ("it's an ideology, not a science"); CEU subsequently was denied accreditation and forced to relocate.[21] Its entire Budapest-based campus was moved to Vienna, Austria. The Orban-led government ramped up its attack on LGBTQ people during the pandemic year, banning adoption by gay couples and stigmatizing transgender children while claiming to "protect" their "right to the gen-

---

21 Franklin Foer, "Victor Orban's War on Intellect," *The Atlantic*, June 2019. Available here: https://www.theatlantic.com/magazine/archive/2019/06/george-soros-viktor-orban-ceu/588070/,

der identity they were born with."²² Interestingly, some far-right governments have coopted the language of postcoloniality, claiming that by fighting "gender ideology" they are fighting against western values. Often, far-right leaders position themselves as militating against multiple imported threats: for instance, both Muslims (a threat from the East) and LGBTQ people (a threat from the West). For instance, Jenny Evang points out that Jaroslaw Kaczynsky, who is known for his hateful rhetoric aimed against Muslim immigrants to Poland also makes LGBTQ people their target. She quotes him saying that gender ideology is "a direct attack on the family and children—the sexualization of children that entire LGBT movement, gender. *This is imported*, but they today actually threaten our identity, our nation, its continuation and therefore the Polish state" (my emphasis).²³ Taking a cue from their far-right leaders, more than 100 Polish cities declared themselves "LGBT-free zones" and adopted aggressive anti-LGBT resolutions.²⁴ A 2019 survey in Poland showed that men under 40 overwhelmingly believed "the LGBT movement and gender ideology" was the "biggest threat facing them in the 21st century"—and not, say, economic inequality, automation, or global warming—effectively demonstrating how one part of the working class can be trained to see another group from the working class as the enemy.²⁵

This brings us to the third reason why LGBTQ oppression persists in the capitalist system: it is an effective way to divide the working class, especially during economically trying times, and is a political tactic. Curiously, this is a Leninist tactic. The scholar of right-wing movements Alexandar Mihailovic showed that when Steve Bannon said in 2016 that he was a Leninist, that wasn't a joke or farce. In his article, "Whither

---

22 Dan Avery, "As the pandemic rages, Hungary ramps up anti-LGBTQ legislation." NBC News Nov 23, 2020. Available here: https://www.nbcnews.com/feature/nbc-out/pandemic-rages-hungary-ramps-anti-lgbtq-legislation-n1248659.

23 Quoted in Jenny Evang, "Is 'Gender Ideology' Western Colonialism? Anti-gender Rhetoric and the Misappropriation of Postcolonial Language," *TQS: Transgender Studies Quarterly* 9.3 (August 2022), 377.

24 Dan Avery, "Joe Biden condemns Poland's 'LGBT-free zones,'" *NBC News* Sep 23, 2020. Available here: https://www.nbcnews.com/feature/nbc-out/joe-biden-condemns-poland-s-lgbt-free-zones-n1240757.

25 Ibid.

the State? Steve Bannon, the Alt Right, and Lenin's State and Revolution,"[26] Mihailovic shows a long legacy of right-wing movement leaders learning from Lenin's tactics and strategies of organizing in order to leverage popular discontent, build pressure, gain power over opponents, with the eventual goal of coming to power. Lenin, in "What is to be Done?" instructs organizers to intervene wherever there is a possibility of worker's struggle, pick up any issue where workers can be agitated, and join them in this agitation. This is, in a way, what the far-right movement builders do, opportunistically, without the Leninist aims. They agitate the workers around a select set of issues where they find that the workers can be agitated, globally, and in an organized way—not against the class enemy, but against each other; not to foment unity, but to sow division.

As a result of this agitation, many achievements of LGBTQ liberation movements have already been reversed. We are seeing a rollback of hard-won protections for LGBTQ people in healthcare, the military, education, and social services. The rollback is extensive: in many US states (and globally), trans people are denied gender-affirming care that they previously had. In the US, trans people were banned from serving in the military; judges with a history of anti-LGBT rulings were nominated to serve in the US judicial system; protection of transgender students under the Title IX law was withdrawn; homeless shelters are allowed to discriminate against homeless LGBTQ people; and healthcare providers are allowed to discriminate against their trans/queer patients.

Towards LGBTQ Liberation

What conclusions can we draw from all this? Can we hope that LGBTQ oppression disappears under socialism? Yes and no: and the arguments outlined above explain why. Residual forms of oppression have a very long half-life; since they predate capitalism, we cannot hope that they simply disappear with it. The sex/gender system[27] is particularly pernicious. I grew up in the USSR, a worker state that put in place, early on,

---

26 In *The Future of Lenin: Power, Politics, and Revolution in the 21ˢᵗ Century* (SUNY Press, 2022), 101-124.

27 Gayle Rubin's term, see "The Traffic in Women."

extensive social reproduction networks designed to relieve women of the second shift, and which had a real, palpable effect on women's lives. Yet, women's liberation remained an unfinished project: my college advisor, a philosophy professor, was permitted to make sexist jokes about how there were no women philosophers in history (not true!), and the faces that looked back at me from the photos of the Politburo were all male. And LGBTQ rights were non-existent. In Cuba, the 2022 Family Code—a progressive family law that enshrines the rights of LGBTQ people, multiple parents, the elderly, and children—was the result of a decades-long struggle of LGBTQ organizers. We can't, therefore, hope that a restructuring of social reproduction will eliminate all oppressions entrenched in the sex/gender system. These multiple oppressions will still need to be tackled, one by one. What we can hope for, however, is that in a socialist country these victories, once achieved, will be more lasting: there will be no need to periodically invoke "family values" or divide the working class. Social reproduction will be distributed rather than concentrated within the nuclear family. The Cuban Family Code, after all, is now considered to be the most progressive not just in Latin America, but in the world.[28] With its extension of rights and responsibilities to multiple parents and actual caregivers (replacing rigid "custody rights"), the Code is a step towards recognizing a system of care beyond the nuclear family, and that's good news not just for LGBTQ couples, but for the LGBTQ youth who, as O'Brien claims, often needs access to a wider range of caregivers/ role models than a two-parent family permits.

So how do we best support the dismantling of oppression based on sexuality and gender expression? We struggle against division, we build alternative social reproduction systems, and we actively dismantle the entrenched sex-gender system (heteropatriarchy) we've inherited from the early hierarchical societies. We fight for socialism, and then we fight some more, for complete liberation. Socialist writer April Holcombe writes: "Gender is a central pillar of understanding oneself, a prism

---

28   Buchanan Waller, "Cuba's 2022 Family Code: A Different Model for Social Progress," *Minnesota Journal of Law and Inequality* Nov (2022). Available here: https://lawandinequality.org/2022/11/02/cubas-2022-family-code-a-different-model-for-social-progress/.

through which personality is refracted."²⁹ True liberation, for Marxists, is not just from economic exploitation, but also from all the other forms of oppression, some of which might be "residual." And today, as LGBTQ issues are weaponized in capitalism in very real ways, we organize to defend our right to control our bodies, and to freely express our genders and sexuality; we demand freedom from the poisonous culture predicated on the threat of sexual assault and violence. Now, when the LGBTQ struggle is heating up, it should be at the forefront of the people's collective struggle.

---

29   "The Freedom to Be: Marxism, gender oppression and the struggle for trans liberation," *Marxist Left Review*, Jul 2020. Available here: https://marxistleftreview.org/articles/the-freedom-to-be-marxism-gender-oppression-and-the-struggle-for-trans-liberation/.

CHAPTER 11
SPEAKING LIKE CHILDREN: LINGUISTIC EXODUS FROM CAPITALIST SUBJECT-FORMATION

Richard M. Allen

RICHARD M. ALLEN is an independent scholar based in the American south, whose research focuses on the intersections between Christian thought, critical theory, and continental philosophy—specifically, how conceptualizations of immanence and language aid the struggle for justice. His writing has been featured in the Religious Theory online supplement of the Journal for Cultural & Religious Theory as well as the Hampton Institute.

Truly I tell you, unless you change and become like children, you will never enter the kingdom of heaven.[1]

The praxis of the linguistic animal does not have a definite script, nor does it produce a final outcome, precisely because it continuously retraces anthropogenesis.[2]

Truth and Meaning Today

BY ANY REASONABLE METRIC, I am a bad Marxist, and, admittedly, would not describe myself as such. I never finished reading the first volume of *Capital*, and my affinity with the Marxist ecosystem took a circuitous route, beginning with Christian appropriators of Jacques Derrida, moving through assorted figureheads within twentieth-century critical theory, and generally settling on the Italian *autonomia* movement as a base framework. Similarly, one might also say that I am a bad

---

1   Matthew 18:3 (NRSV)

2   Paolo Virno, *When the Word Becomes Flesh: Language and Human Nature*, trans. G. Mecchia (South Pasadena: Semiotext(e), 2003/2015), 100.

Christian (with which I am more comfortable as a descriptor). I recognize that even in its best possible form, Christianity is troubled by the necessity of supersessionism to its own identity and practice, and supersessionism itself is simply another name for Christianity.[3] Moreover, I tend to bristle at vehement defenses of objectivity within Christian discourse; there is no such thing as "inerrancy," and concepts of "doctrine" or "truth" are almost entirely self-contained, self-sustained elements of a human construct. Certainly, it would be unfair to label oneself as Christian without affirmation of specific theological assumptions. However, orthodoxy is clearly not my strong suit, as I find inventiveness a more enticing approach than acquiescence to the status quo. Truth, at least the sort of truth necessary for liberation, needs more emphasis on potential compared to what has already been said or done. Our present moment, the actually-existing struggle today, is engendered by and constitutive of a myriad of forces that constantly change, so what has already been said or done is *prima facie* no longer wholly applicable; it may certainly be useful in part, yet as a product of a bygone moment, it can only speak so much. In order to lucidly and effectively counter both the structure and effects of oppression, those who struggle must mine the vast fields of potential, of what *is* possible by definition, in order to fashion something wholly true *today*.

One underlying concern common to any iteration of liberative thought and practice is that of how to exit, let alone overcome, an oppressive structure or environment. What tools, paths, and ideas aid the struggle for liberation, the exodus from captivity? Or, more succinctly, how do we actualize liberation?[4] The answer to these questions will

---

[3] In short, supersessionism is the notion that the Christian church has replaced, or superseded, the Jewish synagogue insofar as communal structure, and by proxy, Christian identity has replaced Jewish identity insofar as God's "chosen" people. Jews are simultaneously excluded from the benefit of salvation by their lack of belief in Jesus as the promised Messiah, yet are still included in the *logic* of salvation as what enables Christianity to be anything at all; without the history and ritual identity of the Jewish people, Christianity could not exist, however Jewish history and ritual now only function to enable Christian order. I am indebted to Timothy Snediker in particular for helping me understand both the force and structure of supersessionism.

[4] In this piece I use "oppression" interchangeably with "capitalism." Oppression can take form vis-à-vis capitalism; capitalism itself is and always will be a form of oppression.

mirror the form of the problem, which is to say, inasmuch as oppression takes material form within the world, so too will liberation. Oppression affects our consciousness and our bodies; it is wholly sensible. Therefore, oppression changes the material nature of our existence, and as such, liberation will respond similarly. One cannot philosophize their way out of oppression alone, nor can one effectively understand the form of oppression in question without philosophical acuity. Returning to the question above—how to exit, let alone overcome, an oppressive environment—it seems clear that a turn toward whatever constitutes "orthodoxy" is not necessarily the wisest option. This is not to suggest that what has been said or done before holds no value, but it is to emphasize that a turn toward inventiveness, the process of creating "new" truth vis-à-vis the field of pure potentiality carries within itself a greater capacity for liberation.

The struggle for liberation is therefore an "immanent relay" between the conceptualization of oppression and the response—the particular iteration of language—to the *form* of oppression.[5] Inasmuch as oppression both appropriates and restricts the linguistic capacity of the subject, so too does the subject always already possess the capacity to respond in a way that subverts the supposed authority of the oppressor. *In other words, language itself is a site of struggle.* And yet, it is not immediately clear how the subject should understand their linguistic capacity, nor what is required to actualize that capacity toward liberative ends. We need a better understanding of the relay between the potential to speak and the act of speaking, as well as an understanding of how oppression—specifically, neoliberal capitalism—restricts the linguistic capacity and function of the subject.

Through the respective works of Italian philosopher Paolo Virno, and educational theorist and activist Derek R. Ford, I hope to illustrate the way in which linguistically "becoming like children" is itself a form

---

5   The concept of "immanent relay" is one I derived from the work of Daniel Colucciello Barber, primarily in his book *On Diaspora: Christianity, Religion, and Secularity* (Eugene: Cascade Books, 2011). Barber's research primarily focuses on the relationship between immanence and transcendence insofar as the question of religion is concerned. Here, I use the concept of an immanent relay to describe a movement between two elements or functions, neither of which are transcendent to the other, but each of which immanently "constitute" the other.

of liberation, or exodus, from the subject-formation-oppression inherent to capitalism. In order to struggle effectively against oppression, the subject must thoroughly recognize what happens in the act of speech, and like children, recognize their innate ability to change the world through that act of speech. It is through the childlike expression of language that one can make an exodus from the radical individualization of capitalism.

Speech, Performance, and Power

A preliminary question: *What occurs in the act of speaking?* At face value, the answer may seem obvious—vocalized sounds, intelligible or otherwise, are emitted by the subject. However, there is also a simultaneous harnessing and renourishment of the potential, or the ability, to speak. For Virno—in a hybrid agreement and critique of Ferdinand de Saussure—the act of speech ("enunciation") and the potential to speak ("ability") are immanently constitutive of each other: the potential to speak produces the act of speaking, and the act of speaking reproduces the potential to speak, *ad infinitum*. In this relay of immanence, the subject exercises a particular mode of power.

> The fact-of-speaking cannot be reduced either to the communicative act that is taking place (the *parole*), or to its virtual prefiguration within the *langue as system*: rather, it shows by means of a single enunciation that we have the *ability* to speak, the *power* to say something [...] Ability on one side, language and enunciation on the other: these are the two inseparable sides of the same page.[6]

Virno continues by offering another bifurcation in his analysis of language: what-we-say and fact-of-speaking, each of which articulates a different relation of the subject to the world. While what-we-say "represents or institutes a worldly state of affairs," the fact-of-speaking "shows language's insertion into the world as context or background for all states of things and enunciations."[7] Another way of explaining these two elements is that what-we-say represents, or describes, the world as it is, while the fact-of-speaking is the "prefigured" milieu of the capacity to speak, of language itself, through which both the possibilities of

---

6   Virno, *When the Word Becomes Flesh*, 44; emphasis in the original.

7   Ibid., 44.

the world itself and all possible utterances are contained. Thus, when the subject speaks, they are not only communicating in a cognitive sense (what-we-say) but in actuality, they are performing a *rite*, the cognitive-communicative utterance, which is necessarily contained within a broader *ritual*, namely, language itself (the fact-of-speaking). It is the fact-of-speaking which "founds and shows the ritual character of our speech," by bearing "witness to the generic power to speak via a single, semantically determined *dictum*."[8] The potential to speak is inexhaustible, constantly renourished vis-à-vis the act of speaking. In the act of speech, there is a cognitive-communicative utterance (what-we-say) and a prefigured background or context through which the world itself and all possible utterances are constituted (fact-of-speaking). While the fact-of-speaking encompasses and necessarily includes what-we-say, it is only the fact-of-speaking which demonstrates the ritualistic character of discourse.

However, for our purposes, what is important to note is that in this immanently constitutive relay between potential and act (whether as *langue* or *parole*, or the fact-of-speaking and what-we-say), the subject exercises a particular mode of power. This power, put simply, is the production, or the "phenomenon," of the speaker—anthropogenesis.

> We call "ritual," then, the empirical experience of transcendence, the discursive evocation of the biological disposition underlying all human speech... Rite is a praxis, and not a conceptual inquiry. The production of an enunciation (not its text) allows the speaker to manifest herself, it literally makes her visible... With the simple emission of an articulated voice—or by positioning herself on the threshold between language and speech, which amounts to the same thing—the speaker becomes a phenomenon, something to which we can attribute a *phainestai*, an appearance. S/he exposes herself to the others' eyes. And it is in this exposition that we find the unmistakable work of the rite.[9]

Virno uses the mediopassive form of the Greek word *phaínō*, or *phenomenon*, to indicate more clearly what happens in the appearance of the subject. It is not simply that upon speaking the subject appears, in the sense of *past* act and *present* appearance, but instead that the performance of the rite of speaking immanently constitutes and affects the

---

8   Ibid., 46; emphasis in the original.

9   Ibid., emphasis in the original.

subject. Put differently, instead of thinking of this appearance in a linear sense, one must think of appearance in a cyclical sense, or as we have seen above, a relay. The rite of speaking makes the subject appear (what-we-say), which reproduces the ritual of language (the fact-of-speaking), giving *truth* to the subject's appearance and *meaning* to the rite of speaking (the power in the production of the subject). This cyclical process is anthropogenesis. Truth is located in the observable fact of the appearance of the subject, and meaning is found in the immanent relay between the rite of speaking and the ritual of language, or anthropogenesis as such. Or, we may say that meaning, for the speaking-subject, derives from the *fact-of-appearing* (truth), a fact which, in its purest form, is *self-produced* vis-à-vis the act of speaking. Meaning is quite simply that the truth of a subject (re)producing themselves is not merely possible but presently occurring as the subject speaks. Inasmuch as the subject exercises anthropogenesis through the reproduction of the potential to speak, they also exercise the generation of truth through the reproduction of anthropogenesis, and it is through these respective relays that meaning itself arises.

Language is therefore ritualistically performative, in which the speaker "officiates" a rite, similar to a priest officiating a spiritual function, or the virtuosity of a musician or actor, respectively performing with an instrument or becoming another character. Through the performative act, the speaker brings to presence the power of language's potential as they speak, and it is through the potential to speak that the speaker (re)produces themselves. This is the phenomenon with which Virno is concerned, that of anthropogenesis, the power of becoming-oneself, or more forcefully, the *power-to-produce-oneself*. If the ritual of language, exercised or officiated through the rite of speaking, is what constitutes both the subject and the world itself, then it is crucial to recognize the potency of this power. Only the subject is intrinsically capable of actualizing and reproducing these immanent relays; truth and meaning are therefore always-already within the grasp of the subject. Without a holistic recognition of anthropogenic power, exercised through the ritual of language, the subject will find their struggle for liberation more challenging, because they are not yet exercising the fullness of the productive—that is to say, anthropogenic—power of language. Truth, the sort of truth the oppressed need to counter whatever might pass for orthodoxy in their moment, must be produced, and it cannot appear unless the subject first appears by performing the rite of speaking, (re)producing themselves as a factual phenomenon of power. The *power-to-produce-oneself* is the *power-to-produce-truth;* anthropogenesis is truth-production.

Childhood and Exodus—Or, Proximity to the Power of Language

We began by elucidating what occurs in the act of speaking. The act of speaking is a rite that cyclically produces both the subject and the ritual of language. As the subject speaks they exercise and constitute the power-to-produce themselves, which simultaneously exercises and constitutes the power-to-produce truth. Meaning can therefore be located in the relay between potential and act, between the fact-of-speaking and what-we say. It is in these respective immanently constitutive relays that the subject produces truth and meaning in the world, but as mentioned previously, truth and meaning must also be considered in a non-linear, cyclical sense. It is this power, which, in its most potent form, reproduces the subject in a way that counters the subject-forming structures of the world. When the subject performs the act of speaking, they present or manifest themselves within and to the world; this production of the subject is anthropogenesis, and the power within anthropogenesis is what contains the potential to constitute, and therefore change, the subject and the world. It is how the subject presents themselves as a subject, or how they "individualize" themselves. Behind any form of language (intelligible or otherwise) there lies a space of limitless potential, the potential for speech, which cannot be exhausted. If the subject, let alone the multitude, understands the power of potential then they can more easily produce new speech to actualize liberation, and similarly, produce new truth to counter the static nature of orthodoxy, or the logic and structures of the world which engender repetition of the same. However, it is not immediately clear how the subject, who has long-since learned to speak in general, can effectively perform the rite of speaking in the ways described above. For this, we will need to work through the concept and experience of childhood, specifically in the acquisition and learning of language, in order to recognize what is possible in the proximity to the power of language as anthropogenic. Here, alongside Virno, we will incorporate the insights of educator and activist Derek R. Ford.

Aligned with his earlier treatment of the relationship between the potential for speech and the act of speech, Virno reaffirms the same insofar as a child's early use of language is concerned. "The child, when verbally announcing what he or she is doing, is not describing an action, but completes a secondary, auxiliary action (the production of an enunciation), whose goal is the visibility of its subject."[10] As the child learns to speak, they are closest in proximity to the potential of language itself, because they have not yet encountered the arbitrary boundary lines of what speech-acts are considered permissible or acceptable. Or, we may say that for the child, the potential of language is akin to that of a playground, in which they have unbridled access to a limitless combination of vocalized sounds from which to *make themselves appear.* If, as Virno states, the goal of the speech-act is the "visibility of the subject," then in childhood the speaking-subject makes themselves visible in the purest manner possible. The purity of their experience of the potential to speak is because of their *proximity* to potential as such. However, as the child ages into adulthood, they gradually encounter the logic and structure of the world, which, animated by neoliberal capitalism, determines for the subject what speech-acts are permissible toward arbitrary ends. This determination by the world-structure is what appropriates the subject-production of language for its own ends, and distances the subject from their proximity to the boundless playground of the potential to speak. Put differently, by the time the subject has progressed beyond childhood, they will find it increasingly difficult to actualize the power-to-produce themselves because they have been driven further away from their proximity to potential; truth and meaning become increasingly abstract and fractured, and the (re)production of the subject becomes the (re)production of what has been said or done before. The speaking-subject must now retrace their steps, so to speak, to relearn the anthropogenic power of language.

Using Virno's analysis of potential, performance, and Marx's concept of the "general intellect," Ford suggests an "exodus" from subjectiv-

---

10   Ibid., 63.

ity as such, toward a "de-individualized," fugitive retreat from capitalism.[11] He characterizes Virno's reinterpretation of the "general intellect" in Marx's writings as pure potential rather than "particular knowledges and thoughts."[12] Thus, instead of thinking only of the *form* of the general intellect, we must consider the capacity by which the general intellect is formed in the first place. It is not so much *what* the multitude says in common (although this is certainly important) but rather *how* the multitude says anything in common, and what forces aid or impede this potential of the general intellect as articulated by both Virno and Ford. Therefore, recognizing a space wherein praxis finds its potential before actualization allows for a renewed understanding of how much power the oppressed have in the pursuit of liberation or "exodus." This power in the relationship between potential and praxis is the same as that of the capacity to speak and the speech-act itself described above. If the subject remains aware that their speech does not ever touch the boundary lines of pure potential, which lies in wait before the utterance, then they can find new ways of living and being through the field of potential, boundless and unformed as it is. This, as we have seen, is anthropogenesis, the power of producing oneself by performing the ritual of language. Yet, in order to more clearly see the usefulness of said potential, we must all undergo "desubjectification," and it is here that Ford's articulation of childhood and language is helpful. He writes:

Through the acquisition of language, the child is separated from their surroundings through individuation, hence the significance of "I speak." By learning language, we encounter the disjuncture between the world and ourselves because we discover that we can change the world and that the world can change us."[13]

Through childhood and the development of our linguistic faculties, we undergo conscious and unconscious individualization, a gradual understanding of our distinction from the world even as we recognize our place within it and its effects upon our life. The struggle, however, arises in the ways capitalism forms our respective identities or individ-

---

11 Derek R. Ford, "The Aesthetics of Exodus: Virno and Lyotard on Art, Timbre, and the General Intellect," *Cultural Politics* 16, no. 2 (2020): 253-269.

12 Ibid., 254.

13 Ibid., 266.

ualization as we practice the act of speech. This conditioning teaches us prescriptive or authoritative ways of speech which only serve to reify existing structures and assumptions. Capitalism prescribes limits to what speech is acceptable or useful toward the acceleration of capital accumulation, and the limits necessarily distract the subject, let alone the multitude, from recognizing the radical immanence of anthropogenic potential in language itself. They are led to believe that they do not possess any genuine capacity to speak, for that capacity is given by and for capital accumulation. If left unchecked, this then accelerates a distinctly *capitalist individualization*, which cannot permit the subject from exercising the fullness of anthropogenesis within a broader community or multitude, as capitalism thrives upon the fracture between the individual and community in order to extract individual labor power more efficiently.

Thus, while in a general sense despite these oppressive restrictions upon the way in which the subject speaks under capitalism, the subject never truly loses access to pure potential behind the utterance, exodus allows us to retreat from the confines of capital in order to learn new ways of speaking. The way out is through a regression of sorts, or a "de-individualization," a return to childhood. As capitalism constantly mutates in order to maintain its structural control, so too should the oppressed—using language offered at the onset of this piece—mirror the form of the problem, by refusing the lie of truth or orthodoxy as static and learning new ways of speaking to undo the linguistic subject-formation of capitalism and exert the power of anthropogenesis. In Ford's words, "As children, we become open to the world beyond its current configuration, and we're capable of—or more accurately, species bound—to learn again and again, differently each time."[14] For Virno as well as Ford, language itself is praxis, and the praxis of language is what draws upon and reproduces anthropogenesis. Yet, since the power of anthropogenesis resides in the immanent relay between the potential to speak and the speech-act itself, without an exodus from the prescribed orthodoxy of capitalism, we will never actualize the radical capacity of language to speak something new, something that could form the subject differently so as to overcome oppression. Practically, for the speak-

---

14   Ibid.

ing-subject, childhood is therefore exodus; it is the positive regression over and against the linguistic structures of capitalism by learning to speak anew, which "retraces anthropogenesis."[15] Exodus is a simultaneous refusal to repeat what-we-say underneath the logic of capitalism and an affirmation of the fact-of-speaking's power to (re)produce the subject over and against any arbitrary boundary. Exodus is childhood reconceptualized for the speaking-subject who has learned to speak in general, a path toward the purity of proximity to the playground of language, the potency of truth and meaning made real *by and for the speaking-subject alone.*

At the beginning of this writing, I cited Jesus' words to his disciples in the Gospel of Matthew. In the narrative, when asked who deserves recognition as the "greatest" in the kingdom of heaven, Jesus responds with a seemingly odd analogy. Bringing a child to his side, Jesus instructs his disciples that unless they *change and become* like little children, they will remain unable to see, let alone experience, the kingdom of heaven. In Christian theology, the kingdom of heaven represents what the world will become as humanity turns toward both God and neighbor in love, and broadly speaking, the kingdom of heaven is considered a restoration of the world to its original good form before the structural effects of human sin took root. Furthermore, it is simultaneously described as "at hand" (which is to say, encountering the world in the present) and also "to come" (inasmuch as it is available to the world in some form, it is not yet fully realizable). At first glance, Jesus' words above seem to refer to obvious differences in societal status—the child being one of the "smallest" or least significant members of society—as a way to highlight the necessity of humility when responding to the divine. However, in light of what Ford and Virno suggest in reference to childhood, we see an expanded materialist vision of the spiritual insight offered by Jesus. Childhood is not merely a state of simple humility, although it includes this dimension. Instead, childhood is the closest any of us come to understanding and accessing the pure potential of being. The question here for Jesus' disciples is that in order to enter the kingdom of heaven, something must change in both their proximity to the potential of being and their (re)production of being in the world. They cannot en-

---

15   Virno, *When the Word Becomes Flesh*, 100.

ter it through their present *form-of-being*, nor through the prescribed *formation-of-being* determined by the world. For Jesus, the child represents the innocence of being human, the purity of potential itself and what happens when the subject is closest to the proverbial playground of being, to which all humans have access but struggle in actualizing. Thus, to enter the kingdom of heaven is to change and become like a child, to leave behind the subject-formations of the world and exercise the productive potential of being, of love itself. One might say that the kingdom of heaven is an immanent relay between the potential for love and the love-act itself. Similar to the relay between the potential to speak and the speech-act itself, which (re)produces the subject and truth *in the world*, the power of the kingdom of heaven is the phenomenon of *subjects* (re)producing themselves and love *for the world*. Or, more forcefully, if the ritual of language is anthropogenesis, then the ritual of the kingdom of heaven is what I label *communigenesis*, both of which work in tandem to restructure the world.

This, I contend, is the power of the exodus and childhood. The lone individual underneath capitalism cannot, on their own, undo structural oppression. However, the individual can first undergo exodus in their understanding and exertion of the capacity to speak, returning to a state of childhood in their closeness to said potential. It is in being proximally closest to the purity of potential that the speaking-subject can recognize the power by which they produce themselves in the world through the rite of speaking, and learn to speak differently, thereby (re)producing themselves in a way undetermined by the world. This is what we mean by anthropogenesis, the immanently constitutive relay between the potential to speak and the act of speech itself. Moreover, as individuals recognize others undergoing exodus toward the state of childhood, they can organize themselves, speaking *together* and (re)producing ways of *being-together* undetermined by the structural logic of the world of capitalism as such. This is what we mean by communigenesis. Without the transition from anthropogenesis to communigenesis, the subject-forming and world-forming logic of capitalism cannot be undone. Language is a site of struggle because it is where being-itself is produced. Under the logic and structure of capitalism, being must be produced toward prescriptive ends, namely the extraction of the subject's labor-power toward accelerated capital accumulation. If these prescriptive ends are to be undone, and the world itself made new, then the subject must *produce being differently*, by undergoing an exodus of subjectivity and learning to speak differently. If childhood is where we learn language, then the only way we can actualize liberation under the confines of the world is to learn to speak differently. In the same way that the only way one can "enter" the kingdom of heaven is to become like a child—who in their sheer, as-of-yet unburdened innocence, happily expresses the potential of love toward others—the only way we can "enter" liberation is to become like children in our production of the capacity to speak and to speak differently, thereby (re)producing being itself, reforming the world toward liberative ends.

Thus, a path to liberation can be found through childhood and exodus, leaving behind and stripping away the linguistic strictures of neoliberal capitalism, returning to a state of being closest to the often-untapped potential of language. Here we can more easily learn new words, new phrases, and new public utterances which aid the quest for liberation. Furthermore, as each subject relearns the power of anthropogenesis, and meaning in the truth it produces by and for the subject alone, they can make the transition toward *communigenesis*. This process de-individualizes the subject from the world in order to (re)produce their being and their language differently; the liberation of the individual's potential to speak, to formulate truth and meaning, is the liberation of the community's potential of being, to formulate a world unlike what has been said or done before. As Ford states:

Exodus subverts the dominant ideology of individuality by posing childhood as a project that connects the individual back to the general intellect in its potentiality rather than its potential actualizations.[16]

In short, in order to actualize liberation, we must first retrace our steps and mine the fields of potential we have long forgotten; we must undergo exodus and become like children in order. As mentioned earlier, what passes for orthodoxy, here in particular neoliberal capitalism, tends to reify existing structures and assumptions. Orthodoxy will not save us.

---

16   Ford, "The Aesthetics of Exodus," 267.

What Must Be Done Today?

I have attempted to demonstrate that language is a site of struggle, that in the immanently constitutive relay between the potential to speak and the act of speaking, the subject undergoes anthropogenesis, however underneath capitalism this productive power is oppressively appropriated for its own ends. Anthropogenesis is also the production of truth, the *fact* of the subject producing themselves in the world, and it is therefore the production of meaning, the sensible *experience* of anthropogenesis. By undergoing exodus and recapturing the state of childhood in their relation to language, the subject can learn to speak differently, thereby (re)producing new truths which can effectively undo and counter the oppressive determination of the world.

Today, these ideas could be applied to a broad range of contexts, not least of which is the general state of whatever passes for the "Left" in the United States of America.[17] It would not be unfair to say that the Left seemingly holds virtually no mass power to transform the social, economic, and political structure of the United States. This is not to suggest that the Left does not possess power, nor that they are incapable of exerting power toward liberative ends. However, it is to recognize a problem inhibiting the forcefulness of the Left to counter, let alone overcome, the determinative structure of capitalism in the United States; in other words, there is a fracture in the relay between anthropogenesis and communigenesis as described above. Here, I will offer one possible example of this fracture.

In the United States of America, we are told that the formation of our "political" being is primarily realized through voting in a representative democracy; the subject's vote, their individual, *political* speech-act, (re)produces their being, their *political* capacity to speak. What is this, however, if not an abject fiction? Does the vote actualize the true power of its potential? I suggest that in our present moment, it does not. The vote can only actualize what is permissible within the bound-

---

17   I do not have the space to expand upon the signifier "Left" and all that it does or does not signify. However, for my purposes, I will simply say that the "Left" comprises any movement or organization which views the Democratic Party as equally-constitutive of the current social, economic, and political order inasmuch as the Republican Party, and incapable of achieving the aims of socialism or communism.

ary lines of the determinative structure; as a political speech-act within capitalism, it can only reify what has been said or done before. This is the fracture in the relay between anthropogenesis and communigenesis for the Left. Because the vote, as a rite of the determinative political structure, has no capacity by which to engender new speech nor new truth, the Left cannot truly transition from individuals to community in their performance of political ritual. If the Left seeks to counter and overcome the determinative structure of the United States of America, then what purpose does it serve, really, to *speak in the political language of the determinative structure?* As we have seen above, the transition from anthropogenesis to communigenesis is the speaking-subject learning to speak-together. And yet speaking-together, in the context of the vote, is speaking-together *for the prescribed ends determined by capitalism*. It cannot produce new rites of speech, and thereby new truth to determine new ends for the community, let alone the speaking-subject.

My hope is that the Left can make their own exodus from the determinative ritual of language and draw upon the well of limitless potential available to them. Perhaps, there is an as-of-yet unrealized benefit to being "bad" leftists or Marxists, insofar as their participation (or lack thereof) in the social, economic, and political structures of our day. The allure of orthodoxy is its forestallment of the need for the subject to produce truth and meaning, its suggestion that there could be truth applicable to any given context at any given time, in which truth simply needs to be recapitulated by the subject. However, as we have seen, the material nature of our present moment is constituted and affected by a myriad of forces in a state of constant flux, so what was "true" yesterday will likely not be *wholly* true today, if at all. We must remake the world entirely, and the only path toward this vision is through childlike inventiveness, through the anthropogenic power of language and the "communigenic" power of being, both of which are immanently constitutive relays between potential and act. Through exodus from the world's determination of subjectivity toward the horizon of pure potential, and becoming like children, we have the chance to form ourselves and the world we need, regardless of what orthodoxy might say is permissible.

CHAPTER 12
DEMANDING TO BE:
TRANS YOUTH AND CLASS STRUGGLE

Eli J. Pine

ELI J. PINE is a recent graduate from American University (CAS '23), where they received a BA in sociology and education studies. Their academic interests traverse political theory, queer/trans studies, philosophy, and educational theory. Currently, they are an independent researcher and a restaurant-industry worker based in Washington, D.C. Eli's political home is with the Claudia Jones School for Political Education, a D.C.-based organization focused on building a multi-cultural, working-class movement for socialism.

Introduction: Class-struggle, Contingency, & Conjuncture

FIVE PAGES INTO the sixth chapter of *Capital Vol. I*, Marx begins distinguishing between the valuation of labor-power and that of all other commodities. Whereas the value of other commodities depends on a combination of two elements (namely: variable and constant capital),[1] the value of labor-power itself, writes Marx, "contains a historical and moral element."[2] For Marx, labor is the human process through which we transform the world around us and, thus, ourselves, but under the capitalist mode of production, this capacity is commodified into labor-power. Distinct from other modes of production, the conditions of capitalism subject workers to a market in which we must sell our capacity to labor (i.e., labor-power) for a wage.

---

1   Karl Marx, *Capital Vol II* (London: Penguin Random House, 1992), 209-210. Thank you to Derek Ford for their feedback on this section and guidance throughout the composition of this piece.

2   Marx, *Capital Vol I* (London: Penguin Random House 1991), 275.

As a precondition for labor-power, humans require an evolving web of necessities ranging from basic needs like food, water, and shelter to more complicated ones like entertainment, social bonds, familial structures, and so on. Marx also teaches us that this 'web of necessities' differs from epoch to epoch, location to location, and civilization to civilization. To put this another way, the 'historical and moral element' embedded in the value of labor-power can include everything from topography to war, climate to ideology, or the transformation of economic systems to the psychological effects of those processes, and everything in between. It is by no means an inevitable measure but plays the central role in the fight between classes of people over the means of production. So, if the value of labor-power depends on historical and moral processes that change socially agreed upon understandings, then a primary task in the *class struggle* becomes *expanding* the social idea of what ought to be included in the 'web of necessities' required to reproduce labor-power.[3]

At every moment of the conjuncture, we should ask ourselves about the current state of the class struggle both to situate ourselves in history and to find possible ruptures in the hegemony of the value-form. On the side of the capitalist class, the central goal of the class struggle is to lower the value of labor-power, which increases the rate of exploitation and produces more surplus-value—something they are constantly realizing. But as even a semblance of collective power among the working class diminishes, it is no secret that our task at hand is significantly larger. So what questions must we ask? If history is any indicator, they should include some things like: Where and by whom is the class struggle being advanced? Which political-economic conflicts are centers of contradiction and tension? And, perhaps most importantly, how can the working class harness the contingent nature of the "historical and moral elements" of labor-power's value to work toward socialism?

My aim in this piece is to look at these questions through what I see as two concurrent and significant sites of class struggle: the legal and

---

3   For an instructive elaboration on the class struggle and its relation to the "historical and moral element" of labor-power's value, see Ford and Majidi, "Surplus Value Is the Class Struggle: An Introduction" *Liberation School*, 30 March 2021. Available here: https://www.liberationschool.org/03-what-is-surplus-value-html.

political attacks on trans*[4] youth and the fight against state-sponsored care (e.g., healthcare, education, social programs, etc.).[5] I propose in what follows that a foray into the historical and present state of capitalist power reveals these two ongoing processes to be not simply related but enacted through and strengthened by each other with the goal of eroding democratic processes/institutions, increasing the rate of exploitation, and in the ideological realm, decreasing the total sum of what we, the working class, can expect from our governing structures. On the one hand, I argue that trans people, and trans youth in particular, are especially threatening to capital due to the demands that inhere in the concept of state-sponsored gender-affirming care. On the other, and this will be my final point, I explore the possibilities of convergent solidarities among trans people and care-workers (which are often overlapping categories).

A Note on the Literature

Thus far, attention to anti-trans policies on the academic left has turned to a site of analysis that dates back to Marx and Engel's early writings: the family. Writers like the editorial staff at *Parapraxis Magazine*—the first issue of which is dedicated to the topic—have explored at length the threat that trans people pose to the capitalist, nuclear family structure.[6] For the sake of brevity (and perhaps at the risk of oversimplification), the

---

4   Trans* is used here in an expansive way that incorporates both transgender people—who may identify as transmasculine, transfeminine, M-T-F, F-T-M, etc.—and genderqueer people who may identify as non-binary, gender fluid, two spirit, or any other non-normative gender formation. It also encompasses people who may identify as multiple of the noted gender formations. For more on this, see Tompkins. For the remainder of this essay, I will solely use "trans" with the implication that it is an expansive and expanding concept.

5   Thank you to David L. Reznik for pointing me toward the term 'state-sponsored care' and for his generous feedback on the rest of this essay.

6   Max Fox, "The Traffic in Children," *Parapraxis*, 11 December 2022. Available here: https://www.parapraxismagazine.com/articles/the-traffic-in-children; Joy James, "Maternal (in)Coherence," *Parapraxis*, 21 November 2022. Available here: https://www.parapraxismagazine.com/articles/maternal-incoherence; and M.E. O'Brien, "The Family Problem, Now," *Parapraxis*, 19 June 2023. Available here: https://www.parapraxismagazine.com/articles/the-family-problem-outro

argument is that capitalist exploitation requires a mode of life-making in which gender, sex, race, and class relations are naturalized and mystified by the family form. Transness poses a threat to this organization of social life because it complicates the seemingly 'natural' and 'rigid' definitions of who does what. If man and woman are not stable categories, it becomes harder to interpellate people into believing women, People of Color, and queer people are *naturally* meant to do unpaid labor to uphold capitalist relations of production.

I am quite sympathetic to this stance and find it to be a great source of inspiration, but I think the most compelling and exciting departure from this theorizing can be found in Kay Gabriel's recent *n+1* piece titled, "The Anti-Trans Panic and the Crusade Against Teachers." Gabriel rightly looks to such groups as Moms for Liberty, conservative pundits like Christopher Rufo, Ben Shapiro, and Matt Walsh, and their funders like the Council for National Policy to study the question at the heart of historical materialist analysis: 'why now?' In Gabriel's own words:

> If the organic tension between trans self-determination and family control over social life could have come to a head at any point, it's not clear why political actors with deep pockets and meticulous plans for power chose to gin up moral outrage at the particular moment they did.[7]

So, while the family may very well be the underlying structure through which social and economic conservativism finds one of its many avenues, we must also be discerning in our critiques of the conjuncture to determine why anti-trans reaction is happening at this moment. Thinking with Gabriel, I want to home in on one challenge that trans youth, in particular, pose to capitalist social relations: the *demand* that the state provide the "so-called necessary requirements"—as Marx would have it—that allow trans people *to be*.[8]

---

7   Kay Gabriel, "The Anti-Trans Panic and the Crusade Against Teachers: Kay Gabriel," *n+1*, October 25, 2023, https://nplusonemag.com/online-only/online-only/the-anti-trans-panic-and-the-crusade-against-teachers/.

8   Marx, *Capital Vol I*, 275.

Historicizing the Conjuncture: A Short History of Political-Economic Forces

With an eye towards the historical materialism that Gabriel asks of us, the following section reviews some of the historical processes that mirror and have led to the current conditions. While publicly carried out by state legislators, governors, and attorneys general, Maggie Astor of the *New York Times* traces most anti-trans state policy to a few right-wing interest groups like the Heritage Foundation, the Alliance Defending Freedom, the Family Policy Alliance (the lobbying wing of Focus on the Family), and the American Principles Project.[9] A quick journey to the webpages of each organization reveals that their shared policy objectives include positions like expanding school choice, promoting traditional Christian and family values, advocating for 'classical' education, fighting 'gender ideology' in schools, and resisting union organizing. Notably, these four groups are primarily funded by capitalist enterprises like the Charles Koch Foundation/Institute, the Ed Uihlein Family Foundation, the Adolf Coors Foundation, and the DeVos's family foundations, among countless other conservative, private/family capitals.[10]

For these family firms and interest groups, political actions against state-sponsored care and trans youth are not primarily about religion but rather, as Joanna Wuest argues, "driven by a corporate money-fueled movement masquerading as a religious liberty one."[11] Whereas

---

9 Maggie Astor, "G.O.P. State Lawmakers Push a Growing Wave of Anti-Transgender Bills," *New York Times*, January 25, 2023, https://www.nytimes.com/2023/01/25/us/politics/transgender-laws-republicans.html.

10 "The Heritage Foundation: A Think Tank on a Mission to Destroy the Public Postal Service," *American Postal Workers Union*, September 1, 2017, https://apwu.org/news/heritage-foundation-think-tank-mission-destroy-public-postal-service; Susan B. Ridgely, "Betsy Devos, Focus on the Family, and Our Public Schools," The Gender Policy Report, February 6, 2017, https://genderpolicyreport.umn.edu/betsy-devos-focus-on-the-family-and-our-public-schools/; Andrew Atterbury, "National Conservative Groups Pour Money into Local School Board Races," POLITICO, September 9, 2022, https://www.politico.com/news/2022/09/19/conservative-school-board-fundraising-florida-00057325; David Armiak, "Koch Spent Nearly $150 Million in 2020 to Extend His Influence and Promote His Agenda," EXPOSEDbyCMD, November 29, 2021, https://www.exposedbycmd.org/2021/11/29/koch-spent-nearly-150-million-2020.

11 Joanna Wuest, "State, Economy, & LGBTQ+ Civil Rights," *Law and Po-*

these contingencies label themselves defenders of Christian doctrine, traditional family values, and American ideals—much of which is true—their primary objective is to increase the rate of surplus-value extracted from labor. Furthermore, the process they are carrying out is the culmination of a decades-long counterrevolutionary movement that began in the mid-20th century in response to domestic and international movements for liberation, decolonization, and socialism. It might seem roundabout, but much of the current moment can be traced back to Supreme Court Justice and corporate executive Lewis F. Powell Jr., whose infamous letter to the US Chamber of Commerce—originally titled "Attack on American Free Enterprise System"—helped foment the rightist political moment of today.

The Powell Memo and the Present

Derek R. Ford aptly explains the "Powell Memo" as a "right-wing counteroffensive against domestic people's movements" that sought to further entrench corporate-personhood, capitalist power, and anti-communist interests in the fabric of the US state.[12] For Powell, the threat of 'leftist', 'revolutionary', and/or 'nationalist' movements in the US was not the problem per se, but it was their 'outsized influence' on college campuses that threatened bourgeois democracy the most. He, like many other conservatives, saw the *demands* of minoritized students in the academy as antithetical to "respectable elements of society" like the university.[13] Pushes for ethnic studies, working-class representation, feminist studies, queer spaces, etc. all appeared to Powell as "demands for social chaos that would threaten the 'free enterprise system' and 'the American political system of democracy.'"[14]

---

litical Economy Project, February 2, 2022, https://lpeproject.org/blog/state-economy-lgbtq-civil-rights/.

12 Derek R. Ford, "The 'Powell Memo' and the Supreme Court: A Counteroffensive against the Many," *Liberation School*, April 6, 2023, https://www.liberationschool.org/powell-memo-supreme-court-counteroffensive/.

13 Ibid.

14 Roderick A. Ferguson, *We demand: The University and Student Protests*, Berkeley, CA: University Of California Press, 2017, 37.

In fact, as Roderick A. Ferguson notes in his book *We Demand: The University and Student Protests*, Powell explicitly urged members of the Chamber of Commerce to promote "'equal time' on the campus speaking circuit for 'individuals or organizations who appeared in support of the American system of government and business.'"[15] Of course, "equal time" was a euphemism for 'a monopoly of time,' and so continued, with different strategy, one part of the project that Eugene McCarthy began just two decades prior: to dismantle any influence of Marxist, anti-racist, anti-sexist, and/or anti-heteropatriarchal movements on the ideas of those in the intellectual setting. But Powell did not stop there.

When Nixon appointed him to the Supreme Court in 1972, Powell immediately pursued the goals laid out in his Memo. In one of his first opinions on the Court—just after he had successfully worked to dismantle affirmative action in *Regents of the University of California v. Bakke*—Powell declared that "the inherent worth of the speech in terms of its capacity for informing the public does not depend upon the identity of its source, whether corporation, association, union, or individual."[16] In other words, corporations were now legally protected under the 14th Amendment's Equal Protection Clause and entitled to the laws of free speech that any individual was. Ferguson sums this up well:

> Through the power of the Supreme Court, Powell produced a social world in which corporations were literally understood as life-forms whose rights must be defended against the challenges put to them by actual people.[17]

The reach of the Powell Memo went far beyond the university and ushered in a new political movement that coupled neoliberal economics with social conservatism.[18] Powell, in his pursuit to eliminate egalitarian projects and in his allegiance to capitalist interests, is perhaps the best example we have of someone who embodied such a connection between reactionary social policies and their economic basis in neoliberalism.

---

15   Ibid, 43-44.

16   First National Bank of Boston v. Bellotti, 435 U.S. 765 (1978).

17   Ferguson, *We Demand*, 42.

18   For a broad and excellent investigation of this convergence, see Cooper's (2017) *Family Values*.

Indeed, the political and judicial opinions that Powell laid out in his memorandum to business leaders went on to form the bedrock ideologies of think tanks like the Heritage Foundation, the CATO Institute, and the Manhattan Institute for Policy Research, among many other conservative institutions.[19] As Melinda Cooper argues in her book *Family Values: Between Neoliberalism and the New Social Conservatism*, the turn to think tanks like the aforementioned marked an important political *and* economic transition from the welfare-state consensus (i.e., Keynesian economics) to the contemporary neoliberal era in which the enclosure of the commons is an increasingly successful project.[20]

It is in this milieu that we find ourselves today, with a deeply neoliberal economy that continues to strip workers of their few-remaining rights and a convergent social conservative movement that uses the think-tank-industrial complex established by Powell and his contemporaries to carry out its fascist goals. There are, of course, endless legislative examples from almost every state in the union that illustrate this vast network of rightist forces. But there is one state in particular that accomplished the gold standard for a policy that encapsulates both anti-trans and anti-care goals at once. Here I want to turn to a policy that Texas governor Greg Abbott's administration implemented through judicial opinion.

Two Birds, One Stone: Opinion No. KP-0401

In February of 2022, Texas Attorney General Ken Paxton responded to a request by then- State Representative Matt Krause, who asked "whether certain medical procedures performed on children constitute child abuse."[21] He was referring to gender-affirming healthcare like puberty blockers and top and bottom surgery. This request circumvented a democratic legislative process, opting instead for the use of the (far less dem-

---

19   Gary Gerstle, *The Rise And Fall Of The Neoliberal Order: America And The World In The Free Market Era*, New York, NY: Oxford University Press, 2022, 108-110.

20   Melinda Cooper, *Family values: Between Neoliberalism and the New Social Conservatism*. New York: Zone Books, 2017, 63-66. Also see Slater (2014) for more on the enclosure of the commons.

21   Office of the Attorney General of Texas, Opinion No. KP-0401, (2022): 1, https://texasattorneygeneral.gov/sites/default/files/global/KP-0401.pdf.

ocratic) judicial branch to determine whether or not gender-affirming care falls under the Texas penal code's definition of child abuse.

In order to issue Opinion No. KP-0401, which asserts that gender-affirming care does indeed legally constitute the abuse of children, Paxton had to first establish a few preconditions. Notably, the first premise, on which the rest of the opinion depends, is that transness is an *impossible* ontological category. He writes clarifyingly, "It remains medically impossible to truly change the sex of an individual because this is determined biologically at conception" and opines that "'sex change' procedures seek to *destroy* a fully functioning sex organ in order to *cosmetically* create the illusion of a sex change."[22] So, for Paxton, the social position of transness is seen as an irrational category that simply does not exist. We can consider this the necessary pretext for interpreting Texas' legal precedent on child abuse, but there is one passage especially relevant to this essay that we must quote at length:

> Courts have analyzed the imposition of *unnecessary* medical procedures upon children in similar circumstances in the past to determine whether doing so constitutes child abuse. One such situation that the law has addressed is often referred to as 'Munchausen by proxy' or 'factitious disorder imposed on another'... In situations such as this, an individual *intentionally* seeks to procure—often by *deceptive* means, such as *exaggeration*—*unnecessary* medical procedures or treatments either for themselves or others, usually their children. In Texas, courts have found that these 'Munchausen by proxy' situations can constitute child abuse... In the context of elective sex change procedures for minors, the Legislature has not provided any avenue for parental consent, and no judicial avenue exists for the child to proceed with these procedures and treatments without parental consent.[23]

In this passage, the use of the legal metaphor "Munchausen by proxy" undergirds the entire claim of KP-0401 (i.e., that adults who support gender-affirming care for trans youth are committing an act of child abuse)

To shine some light on the metaphor, "Munchausen by proxy"—

---

22   Ibid., 2-3, emphasis my own.

23   Ibid., 7-8 (emphasis my own).

now called 'factitious disorder imposed on another'—has a troubling history. Kanaan and Wessely argue that the diagnosis is merely an evolution of other ideological obfuscations like 'malingering' and 'hysteria,' which have historically served as a means of quelling insurgence by responding to refusals to work and to accept patriarchy (respectively) with medicalization.[24] When people express egalitarian demands, in other words, it is common for the legal- and medical-industrial complexes to insist that they are only conveyed from a place of insanity or mental illness. Furthermore, words like 'unnecessary', 'exaggeration', and 'deceptive' point to the struggle over what is considered a "necessary requirement" to live. If trans youth are seen as victims of something akin to Munchausen by proxy, the justification for this is that they are seeking unnecessary, exaggerated, and deceptive care from the state. Under Texas law, then, any adult supporting medical transition *must* be imposing a disorder, and therefore abusing children. This has particular and drastic effects on the ability of care-workers to do their jobs.

Think, for a minute, about the role of a good teacher, for example. What first comes to mind is the ability to foster positive, supportive, and trusting relationships with students. Now, imagine there is a trans student in this hypothetical classroom who has asked for support with their journey of medical transition. A good teacher, with the necessary qualifications, should be able to offer guidance, emotional aid, and other forms of care. Should said teacher do so, however, Opinion No. KP-0401 dictates that they can and *will* be held responsible for child abuse under the Texas law. The outcome of this situation is the same when applied to any other care-provider. In fact, the opinion explicitly refers to "teachers, nurses, doctors, day-care employees, employees of a clinic or health care facility that provides reproductive services, juvenile probation officers, and juvenile detention or correctional officers"[25] as the primary targets of the law. The goal, then, of KP-0401, is not just to create legal precedence for outlawing trans identity but to set parameters on the essential and fundamental duties of the care-workers who make it

---

24 Richard A.A. Kanaan, and Simon C. Wessely, "The Origins of Factitious Disorder," *History of the Human Sciences* 23, no. 2 (2010): 68–85, https://doi.org/10.1177/0952695109357128.

25 Texas Att'y General Opinion No. KP-0401, (2022): 12, https://texasattorneygeneral.gov/sites/default/files/global/KP-0401.pdf.

possible to reproduce life as we know it.

Necessary Requirements, Habits, and Expectations of the Working Class

Here I want to return to Marx's idea of labor-power's value within the capitalist mode of production. In a word, the "so-called necessary requirements" that Marx discusses in the sixth chapter of *Vol I.* are the historically- and geopolitically-contingent needs that I mentioned in the introduction (e.g., social bonds, entertainment, familial structures, etc.). To get more specific, Marx writes:

[The owner of labour-power's] *natural* needs, such as food, clothing, fuel and housing vary according to the climatic and other physical peculiarities of his country. On the other hand, the number and extent of his *so-called necessary requirements*, as also the manner in which they are satisfied, are themselves products of history, and depend therefore to a great extent on the level of civilization attained by a country; in particular they depend on the conditions in which, and consequently on the habits and expectations with which, the class of free workers has been formed.[26]

In this formulation, which proceeds the one I've quoted in the introduction, Marx is reflecting on how the value of labor-power is measured under the capitalist mode of production. Similarly to Marx's labor theory of value, the measure of labor-power's value must incorporate the things that make possible the reproduction of life. But he also troubles the distinction between 'natural needs' and 'so-called necessary requirements' by implying that a civilized society is one in which the 'so-called necessary requirements' of the proletariat are prioritized to a great extent.

Furthermore, and most relevant to this essay, Marx argues that the requirements of the working class "depend on the conditions in which, and… on the habits and expectations with which the class of free workers has been formed."[27] When trans youth submit that state-sponsored, gender-affirming care is the necessary requirement for trans life-making,

26   Marx, *Capital Vol I*, 275, emphasis my own.
27   Ibid.

when their *demands* fundamentally change the 'habits and expectations with which the class of free workers has been formed,' they implicitly call for an increase in the value of labor-power and, hence, threaten the capitalist class's current success in the class-struggle.

Indeed, Marx's insistence that the value of labor-power partially depends on 'the habits and expectations' of the working class illustrates that true state-sponsored care, if realized, would increase the value of labor-power exponentially. This means that an essential component in the clash over the value of labor-power (i.e. the class-struggle) boils down to the battle over what ought to be included in the 'so-called necessary requirements' of life-making. Under capitalism, to be blunt, this is the fight over what allows us *to be*. We can perhaps best think of this as a linear relationship; an increase in the value of labor-power will more than likely expand the possibilities of life-making while a decrease in this value will almost certainly decrease them. Trans-led demands for state-sponsored care fit squarely into this formula because if such a goal is reached, I wager that it would be more possible for trans communities who currently belong to the reserve army of labor to find an upward mobility that exists for so few people in this country. Of course, the effects of racialization and transmisogyny complicate the possibility of equal results in this process, but this is all the more reason for a movement that embraces a universal class politics in which no group of marginalized people is left behind.

Conclusion: Toward a Politics of Life-Making

In the introduction, I introduced the term 'convergent solidarities', which I use, in this case, to describe the process of movement-building between trans communities and care-workers. Recently, for instance, the National Education Association (the largest teacher's union in the US) publicly denounced attacks on trans/queer students and promised to combat any such efforts.[28] Other care-worker unions like National Nurses United have also issues statements condemning attacks on trans

---

28   Madeline Will, "'We Say Gay': Largest Teachers' Union Pledges to Fight Anti-LGBTQ+ Policies," Education Week, July 7, 2023, https://www.edweek.org/teaching-learning/we-say-gay-largest-teachers-union-pledges-to-fight-anti-lgbtq-policies/2023/07.

patients. There are certainly limitations to institutionalized union organizing, but the prospect of a labor-movement that explicitly points to gender justice as an issue of class-warfare is exciting to say the least.

Indeed, a primary task in the current conjuncture must be exposing mystifications like so-called culture wars for what they are: an effort to increase the rate of exploitation of the working class to generate more surplus value for capital. The current rise in legal and political policy that simultaneously dismantles state-sponsored care networks *and* undermines the egalitarian demands of trans youth and communities at large is indicative of a targeted, well-organized, and strategic rightist movement. It started with Powell and is currently continuing through the political infrastructure he built, but the left's priorities in fighting this movement must have a primary focus on highlighting seemingly 'cultural' dynamics *as class politics themselves.*

Throughout this essay, I have argued that the demands of trans youth, who have both led the recent charge for state-sponsored care and been the primary targets of anti-trans policy, should be seen as demands for an increase in the expectations of the working class a whole. I have also tried to show that this requires of the left the type of organization that utilizes demands like these to expand the value of labor-power. Little doubt is left in my mind that this is only one step in building a socialist project that guarantees for all the conditions of life-making, but it is nevertheless a crucial one if we are to see a world in which trans people, workers, and all marginalized communities are given what they need *to be*.

CHAPTER 13
PARTING THOUGHTS
ATTACKING DIFFERENCE, PURSUING UNITY: BUILDING A SOCIALIST MOVEMENT AMIDST A DYNAMIC WORKING CLASS

Sudip Bhattacharya

SUDIP BHATTACHARYA is a doctoral candidate in Political Science at Rutgers University. You can find his written work at *Jacobin*, *Protean* magazine, and *Black Agenda Report*, among other outlets.

As THE UNITED STATES gradually returns to its pre-colonial roots, with a growing non-European majority, it's critical to not fall prey to assumptions, including the belief, shared by progressives such as Steve Phillips, that there is now a progressive constituency lurking.[1] That somehow, due to this increase in non-white representation, mainly due to the increase of Asian and Latinx populations, progressive coalitions shall inevitably emerge, prepared to battle against the powerful.

For those of us invested in systemic change, and in the replacement of capitalist grift with socialist freedom and liberty, clarity is essential. It's worth remembering that a) we've been here before, and b) there are no definite answers without study and reflection. Ultimately, there remains great potential for socialists to organize a favorable constituency since, for most people of color, including those of us who've "made it" into the middle classes, we earn our daily bread and shelter through work, and anyone with a sense of self can at least sense the growing challenges of simply securing some semblance of a "normal" life amidst neo-

---

1 Steve Phillips, *Brown Is the New White: How the Demographic Has Created a New American Majority* (New York: New Press, 2018).

liberal decay and hubris.

Still, organizing a pro-socialist constituency requires socialists to establish an independent party that's willing and able to meet people's short-term needs and directly challenge the influence and power of other entities seeking to appropriate the growing constituency of color for their own ends. Since the rise of Reaganism and Clintonian "third way" strangulation, a political void has opened following the repression and failures of the Left, allowing groups and "community leaders" aligned with either party to rush in, convincing people to participate in mainstream politics rather than seek more confrontational means of shifting power (i.e. choosing to register for the 2020 presidential election rather than continuing the street-level protests following the murder of George Floyd).[2]

The radical Assata Shakur, herself a socialist and member of the Black Liberation Army, echoed this analysis during her time organizing and resisting in the late 1960s and early 1970s. Shakur, who admits to being raised a "patriot," shifted her political allegiances from liberal to socialist as she grew more acquainted with other members of the working class.[3] She too grew up in difficult circumstances. But it wasn't until Shakur met African students at American universities and working-class blacks far worse off than her that she began to recognize the necessity of building a radical workers' struggle. That realization led Shakur to visit the West Coast to meet with Asian radicals of the Red Guard, a group that sought to represent working-class and poor Asians in Southern California.

"I was especially anxious to meet up with them because it was so hard to get information about them back East. The West Coast has the largest Asian population in the country and I really wanted to get a good idea about what was going on in the Asian communities. A lot of people think Asians do not experience racism, that they are professionals and business owners, unaware that many are poor and oppressed," Shakur

---

2   Lester Spence, *Knocking the Hustle* (New York: Punctum Books, 2015); Mike Davis, *Prisoners of the American Dream* (New York: Verso, 2018).

3   Assata Shakur, *Assata: An Autobiography* (Chicago: Lawrence Hill Books, 1987), 139.

wrote.⁴ Even as she was on her own political journey, Shakur knew that the working class was dynamic and needed to be understood as such. This too is something that Marxists and revolutionaries have recognized. Karl Marx himself spoke of the various ethnic, racial, regional, and religious divisions within the working class. Much of that analysis was rooted in his disappointment and fear of the English working class's reluctance to ally themselves with their Irish counterparts based on their own simmering biases.⁵

Nonetheless, Shakur stressed the need for liberatory movements, however diverse, to never veer off the socialist path. While some scholars are obsessed with difference, believing it precludes universal struggle, Shakur took a different tack. The deeper she sank into the lives of her working-class peers, the more she believed their woes were due to an economic and political system that exploited their labor. Shakur therefore sought a true redistribution of power and resources.

"I got into heated arguments with sisters or brothers who claimed that the oppression of Black people was only a question of race," Shakur wrote.⁶

An effective socialist movement must adopt that same attitude. An appreciation of difference to unite the movement, coupled with a strategy of building a pro-socialist constituency independent of mainstream parties and politics, is what we need to lead lives of dignity and joy.

Progress & Precarity

The formal end of Jim Crow gave way to forms of progress unthinkable in previous decades. A new middle class began to emerge, grow, and build. More opportunities had finally been seized. More migrants from Asia and parts of the globe other than Europe began to find their way to America, becoming part of a new demographic milieu that white su-

---

4   Ibid., 200.

5   Kevin B. Anderson, *Marx at the Margins: On Nationalism, Ethnicity, and Non-Western Societies* (Chicago: University of Chicago Press, 2016).

6   Shakur, *Assata: An Autobiography*, 190.

premacists have been fighting against for generations.⁷

However, despite such gains, the horizons for what was possible quickly dwindled by the mid-to-late 1970s. Why? A constituency of middle-class whites had been mobilized by extremists like Ronald Reagan to oppose necessary expansion of the Great Society/New Deal order. Even the labor movement, which had purged its radical Left, fell in lockstep with a Democratic Party that no longer even pretended to care about social democratic reform.⁸

Soon, a neoliberal consensus had snaked its way into the heart of mainstream politics. By the end of the 1980s, both major parties agreed that society needed to be run like a business rather than something that was at least nominally interested in providing resources for, and being accountable to, the masses. Under this neoliberal consensus, government largesse and control grew, but for the benefit of private enterprise. Instead of finally providing access to housing and healthcare, government provided money and protection to insurance companies and property developers. Most of all, especially with the decline of the labor movement, most people of color, regardless of what collar they wore, needed to work tirelessly just to barely maintain what they already had.⁹

"Blacks, Latinos, and Asians, including immigrants, composed about 15-16 percent of the workers in production, transportation, and material moving occupations as well as in service occupations in 1981 and now make up close to 40 percent of each of these broad occupational groups. Furthermore, these groups are spread throughout these occupational categories to a much larger degree than in the past. In construction trades, for example, workers of color composed 37 percent in 2010, compared to 15-16 percent in 1981… Blacks, Asians, and Latinos together composed about 35 percent of the employed working class, compared to 22 percent for the middle class and 11 percent for the capitalist class," labor reporter and historian Kim Moody noted.¹⁰

7   Erika Lee, *The Making of Asian America: A History* (New York: Simon & Schuster, 2015).

8   Mike Davis, *Prisoners of the American Dream*; Nelson Lichtenstein, *State of the Union* (Princeton: Princeton University Press, 2013).

9   Spence, *Knocking the Hustle*.

10   Kim Moody, *On New Terrain: How Capital is Reshaping the Battleground of Class*

The creation of a predominantly white "middle class" in the postwar era was only possible through government intervention and subsidies. Government programs such as the GI Bill allowed for more whites to attain relative financial stability behind white picket fences and neon green lawns.[11] This was not to be during the 1990s and 2000s, when social programs were gutted, dropping the floor beneath people of color striving for similar levels of economic gain.

Indeed, recent data on social mobility reveals that, as much as people of color have navigated their way into the middle classes, precarity remains the norm. After all, being middle-class doesn't alter the reality that one must work to maintain the privileges they have. It doesn't alter the fact that the global capitalist system itself is far more precarious than it's been in recent memory, with wages lagging behind living costs. A significant percentage of black and Latinx middle-class households vacillate, due to these conditions, between middle and lower-income.[12]

Asian Americans, though oftentimes elevated by pro-capitalists as exemplars of the American Dream, are also in an increasingly precarious economic position. According to the Center for American Progress, the gap between the Asian who earns the most and the Asians who earn the least is now the largest compared to all other major racial/ethnic groups.[13] Across major cities like New York, more and more Asians are part of the growing class of people who are either poor or at least struggling.

"Researchers found that 23% of Asian New Yorkers lived in pover-

---

War (New York: Haymarket, 2017), 35-6.

11   Ira Katznelson, *Fear Itself: The New Deal and the Origins of Our Time* (New York: Liveright, 2013).

12   Rakesh Kochhar and Stella Sechopoulos, "Black and Hispanic Americans, those with less education are more likely to fall out of the middle class each year," *Pew Research*, 10 May 2022, Available here: https://www.pewresearch.org/short-reads/2022/05/10/black-and-hispanic-americans-those-with-less-education-are-more-likely-to-fall-out-of-the-middle-class-each-year.

13   Christian E. Weller and Jeffrey Thompson, "Wealth Inequality Among Asian Americans Greater Than Among Whites," *Center for American Progress*, 20 December 2016, Available here: https://www.americanprogress.org/article/wealth-inequality-among-asian-americans-greater-than-among-whites.

ty in 2020, comparable to the rate of poverty experienced by Black and Latinx New Yorkers, and higher than the citywide average of 16% of all New Yorkers," Chau Lam wrote.[14]

All of this is to say that people of color need socialism. The masses of Asian, African-American, Latinx, and indigenous people would greatly benefit from a classless political system wherein labor is done for the public good and people have what they need to live well—from universal housing to healthcare to recreational resources.

"Complete emancipation of women is possible only under Socialism," said Claudia Jones, one of the leading theoreticians of the Communist Party USA (CPUSA) from the late 1930s into the 1950s. As one of the few black women in leadership, Jones emphasized the centrality of socialism to black and feminist liberation. The Soviet Union, Jones explained, had what women needed to truly be free—from communal kitchens to daycares and more.

"It was only with the October Socialist Revolution that, for the first time in history, women were fully emancipated and guaranteed their full social equality in every phase of life," Jones wrote.[15]

The presence of different elements within the working class should not mystify the obvious: Marxism can provide a system-level answer to what people of color need to be more of themselves in a world that currently holds us back and erodes our sense of being and happiness. While individual-level racism and bigotry can survive even in fully socialist societies (especially during their formative years), socialism is the only project that can handle the system-level problems oppressed groups endure under capitalism or any other regressive system of exploitation and control. It is under capitalism that people of color must work to earn a living. It is capitalism, as Jones noted, that sustained modes of extreme exploitation like Jim Crow, since it elevates into power the most regressive elements in society.[16]

---

14   Chau Lam, "Nearly one in four Asian adults in NYC lived in poverty in 2020: Report," *Gothamist*, 3 May 2022, Available here: https://gothamist.com/news/nearly-one-in-four-asian-adults-in-nyc-lived-in-poverty-in-2020-report.

15   Charisse Burden-Stelly and Jodi Dean, *Organize, Fight & Win: Black Communists Women's Political Writing* (New York: Verso, 2022), 192.

16   Carole Boyce Davies, *Left of Karl Marx: The Political Life of Black Communist*

Even with the increased diversity of the working class, there remain core universal problems and experiences that only socialism can address. Yes, working-class people of color can have differing immediate issues that might separate them at times. But shared conditions like poverty and precarity mean their economic interests remain aligned. Capitalism will never alleviate this common destitution.

Opposition & Co-optation

Although conditions have worsened, and people of color generally are to the left of whites on most issues, it would be naive to believe that a pro-socialist constituency will suddenly develop, like a rose growing from the concrete. Instead, as Antonio Gramsci expressed during the rise of fascism in Italy, crises oftentimes beget more crises. When people are overwhelmed, they retreat into their locus of control, like working more jobs or, perhaps, voting for a particular candidate when told.[17]

In times of great uncertainty, most people usually develop contradictory or confused attitudes and perspectives. As mentioned, Shakur herself admitted to being someone who would've stood for the Pledge of Allegiance when younger and, for a while, even believed in some of the American propaganda around the Vietnam War. This was despite already experiencing oppression first and secondhand.

Similarly, in the past few years, we've witnessed the rise of street rebellion during the George Floyd protests. But we've also seen people of color choosing to vote for candidates like Joe Biden, a man who vociferously opposed desegregation and even eulogized someone as odious as Strom Thurmond—something that other center-right Democrats refused to do.[18] Because of Donald Trump's rise, the growing momen-

---

Claudia Jones (Durham: Duke University Press, 2007), 38.

17   Antonio Gramsci, *Selections from the Prison Notebooks* (New York: International Publishers, 2014).

18   David Von Drehle, "Opinion: Biden will need partners to restore our institutions. Where will he find them?," *The Washington Post*, 27 October 2020, Available here: https://www.washingtonpost.com/opinions/biden-will-need-partners-to-restore-our-institutions-where-will-he-find-them/2020/10/27/11f3f506-186d-11eb-befb-8864259bd2d8_story.html.

tum of the far Right, and the political void on the Left—a void that's existed for generations—most people of color will continue to engage with politics in ways that are counterproductive, and dangerous for our longer-term sanity.

For instance, many African Americans want to change our so-called justice system. And yet they continue to express support for police funding to either remain the same or increase. They support candidates obsessed with "law and order"—center-right Democrats like Mayor of New York Eric Adams and Biden.[19] Asians too, understandably worried by the potential return of Trump and his anti-Asian rhetoric, are sometimes eager to support any Democrat. That's assuming they don't feel alienated from politics entirely.

Among Latinx registered voters (many people of color remain unregistered), a split has re-emerged between those supporting Biden and others more sympathetic to Trump.[20] In some parts of the country such as Texas, one finds Asians also supporting Republican candidates over Democrats.[21] More Asians and Latinx, who supported candidates like Bernie Sanders, remain distant from politics generally. One wonders how they feel following the collapse of the Sanders campaign and his growing ties to the mainstream of the Democratic Party.

Fear, dread, anger, disillusionment with the "system" is never enough. Such feelings and views can melt into nothingness, or spill over into politics that remain contained and contorted. Jones knew this well as, following the end of World War II, the Democratic Party orchestrated a conservative backlash against women who had been recruited to work in industrial jobs when the men were off in Europe and Asia.

---

19   Katie Glueck, "What Does Eric Adams, Working-Class Champion, Mean for the Democrats?," *The New York Times*, 26 June 2021, Available here: https://www.nytimes.com/2021/06/26/nyregion/eric-adams-mayor.html.

20   Rebecca Picciotto, "Trump wipes out Biden's lead with Latino voters in 2024: CNBC survey," *CNBC*, 19 December 2023, Available here: https://www.cnbc.com/2023/12/19/trump-wipes-out-bidens-lead-with-latino-voters-in-2024-cnbc-survey-.html.

21   David Leonhardt, "Asian Americans, Shifting Right," *The New York Times*, 6 March 2023, Available here: https://www.nytimes.com/2023/03/06/briefing/asian-americans-conservative-republican.html.

As Jones noted, women needed socialism, though some expressed frustration with her following some of the "pro-family" policies under Harry Truman, which were really about encouraging domesticity, making it easier for women to be laid off.

"It is clear therefore that in such a situation our Party must correctly assess its own activities as regards work among women, if it is to play its vanguard role in this important sphere of the struggle for peace and progress," Jones stated when discussing the role of the CPUSA in organizing women during the post-war years.[22]

As much as Jones believed in people's capacities to interpret—at some base level—their conditions, she also knew better than to assume frustration would necessarily morph into effective politics. Developing a pro-socialist constituency requires people willing to provide the resources for others to nurture the skills and fortitude to believe in and fight for a better world.

People need funds to alleviate the burdens of daily living under capitalism and foster more freedom to organize for broader policy ambitions. People need political relationships with others around the globe facing similar conditions and invested in similar goals. People need leadership and guidance from those who have experience organizing campaigns. Finally, people need more knowledge about what they are up against, how the system operates, and what kinds of political systems others have tried.

"Our theoretical understanding of the Negro question must be developed in practical day-to-day action, carefully planned and executed. Negro leadership within the Party must be strengthened and broadened, in the interests of a wholesome movement. We must continue the trend in training Negros as Marxist-Leninist teachers, thinkers, and workers within the Party," as Thelma Dale, another black woman radical and CPUSA member, expressed.[23]

After nearly five decades of neoliberal rot, most people of color, and most whites, haven't had much tangible relation to collective move-

---

22 Burden-Stelly and Dean, *Organize, Fight & Win: Black Communists Women's Political Writing*, 174.

23 Ibid., 150.

ments challenging the grip of capitalist power. Instead, most people create their own communities, through sports, food, culture, religion, etc. Some gain meaning through various forms of consumption. Others simply ascertain a sense of self and meaning through recreational drug use.

For some, given that there still isn't much of a Left, their other option is to interact with the Democratic Party or, sometimes, the GOP.

As others have astutely argued, since the rise of neoliberalism, there's been the parallel rise of what's known as a "misleadership" class—people of color whose immediate interests may align with the status quo. Those interests are often class-based.[24] Entrepreneurs of color might market buying their products as a form of racial unity and progress.[25] Those same entrepreneurs, or those who agree with them politically, may define racial justice as more executives or defense contractors of color.

Such counterrevolutionary forces have expanded over the years. As Glen Ford has written about extensively, a network of pro-Democrat "community leaders" and groups have managed to sink their teeth into African-American communities across the nation.[26] They have done the same to Asian Americans. During the latest special election in Georgia, it was progressive civic groups that turned out Asian voters in the suburbs surrounding Atlanta, helping the Democrats win both US Senate seats.[27]

The only way to develop a pro-socialist constituency uniting groups of color across America is to organize people independent of both major parties and their various political extensions. Only through an indepen-

---

24   Eva Dickerson, "How the Black Misleadership Class provides cover to Cop City", *Hammer & Hope*, Summer 2023, Available here: https://hammerandhope.org/article/andre-dickens-cop-city-black-politicians.

25   Adolph Reed, Jr., *Class Notes: Posing as Politics and Other Thoughts on the American Scene* (New York: The New Press, 2000); Keeanga-Yamahtta Taylor, *From #BlackLivesMatter to Black Liberation* (New York: Haymarket, 2019).

26   Glen Ford, *The Black Agenda* (New York: OR Books, 2021).

27   Li Zhou, "Georgia is a perfect example of the growing power of Asian American voters," *Vox*, 28 December 2022, Available here: https://www.vox.com/policy-and-politics/2022/12/28/23519123/georgia-asian-american-voters-turn-out-warnock.

dent socialist endeavor can we build the power and influence our communities deserve and need to improve their lives before the Earth burns to ashes.

But to do so also means taking into account the dynamism of said working class, which is very Asian, Latinx, African-American, white-collar and blue, masculine, feminine, and non-binary. There are material differences among the working class that matter if a movement aims to be strong and capable of replacing capitalism.

For many non-men, reproductive care is essential. As is police reform for many lower-income black and brown communities. Access to citizenship matters greatly to undocumented people. Such concerns must be dealt with and incorporated into the broader fight for resources and rights. Addressing such critical issues will create more space and motivation for oppressed working people to join the struggle against capital.

This was Jones's major insight when it came to organizing women into the CPUSA.

"By connecting the struggle against the seemingly little issue of crowded schoolrooms, unsanitary conditions, lack of child care facilities, etc., with the issues of reactionary content of teaching—racism, jingoism, etc.—the political consciousness of the parent masses can be raised to the understanding of the interconnection between the demand for lunch for a hungry child and the demand of the people for economic security; between the campaign for the dismissal of a Negro-hating, anti-Semitic Mae Quinn from the school system and the fight of the people for democratic rights; between the protest against a jingoistic school text and the broad fight of the people for peace," Jones wrote.[28]

But, again, such differences should be framed as immediate concerns that must be addressed toward the end goal of building a more unified, stronger socialist struggle. This is why we need a socialist party and leadership that can ensure such material differences are dealt with all while not allowing such differences to devolve into fracture, which is always a possibility. As much evidence as there is of Asian, African-Amer-

---

28   Burden-Stelly and Dean, *Organize, Fight & Win: Black Communists Women's Political Writing*, 196.

ican, and Latinx people's willingness to work together, there have also been instances of antagonism.

Prior to African-American and mainly Puerto Rican organizers, who'd been steeped in labor and housing advocacy, trying to bridge divides between their communities in the 1950s in New York City, many African Americans and Puerto Ricans did not see eye to eye. Many African Americans felt Puerto Ricans were more privileged. And many Puerto Ricans, despite their own grinding poverty, refused to believe they faced similar issues as African Americans. What changed the scenario was the work of organizers intent on mobilizing for the critical resources these communities lacked.[29]

In California, following World War II, the assumption resurfaced among progressives that a non-white coalition of Japanese, Mexican, Chinese, and African Americans was about to be unleashed. Instead, divisions festered. Mexican and Chinese Americans were convinced that their issues of language access were being ignored by policymakers in favor of desegregation, which was racially coded as only pertaining to African Americans. Politicians like Reagan swooped in, exploiting such differences to seize just enough Mexican and Chinese-American support to claim the California governorship.[30]

"To win any struggle for liberation, you have to have the way as well as the will, an overall ideology, and strategy that stem from a scientific analysis of history and present conditions," said Shakur in her reiterative assessment of how oppressed and exploited peoples should view political struggle.[31]

There are differences, certainly. The intensity of warfare that the Vietnamese endured under US bombing and cruelty was not exactly the same as the warfare that black and brown people faced within the US. And yet they shared a common enemy and intense level of suffering.

---

29   Sonia Song-Ha Lee, *Building A Latino Civil Rights Movement: Puerto Ricans, African Americans, and the Pursuit of Racial Justice in New York City* (Chapel Hill: The University of North Carolina Press, 2014).

30   Mark Brilliant, *The Color of America Has Changed: How Racial Diversity Shaped Civil Rights Reform in California 1941–1978* (Cambridge: Oxford University Press, 2010).

31   Shakur, *Assata: An Autobiography*, 242.

They also shared a need for a socialist world to be born — for a world in which the US police and military have been abolished and replaced with actual systems of care and accountability rather than grime, pain, and hopelessness.

No Amount of Difference Negates the Necessity of Class War

"In order to play an effective role, we as Communists, will have to extricate ourselves completely from the revisionist way of thinking and acting, and move with dispatch to meet the immediate problems confronting us," Jones once said.[32]

But that hope of a more brilliant future now relies on a Left that is incredibly weak and marginal compared to liberal forces and, of course, the right-wing that seeks our death.

The stakes are high. What will be our collective response?

---

32   Burden-Stelly and Dean, *Organize, Fight & Win: Black Communists Women's Political Writing*, 150.

www.ingramcontent.com/pod-product-compliance
Lightning Source LLC
LaVergne TN
LVHW092104060526
838201LV00047B/1565